A Self-Study Guide for the ISTQB Agile Foundation Exam (CTFL-AT)

Chhavi Raj Dosaj

ISTQB certified registered trainer for ISTQB Foundation Level (CTFL), ISTQB Foundation Level- Agile Tester Extension (CTFL-AT) & ISTQB Advanced Level- Test Manager (CTAL-ATM)

A Self-Study Guide for the ISTQB Agile Foundation Exam (CTFL-AT)

By Chhavi Raj Dosaj

Contents

Acknowledgments

I would like to acknowledge that this book relies heavily on the ISTQB Foundation Agile Level syllabus and ISTQB standard Glossary of Terms. In some cases, certain phrases were used verbatim to ensure the content adheres to the syllabus and glossary.

I would like to thank Arun Kumar for helping me in the preparation of diagrams and Jayshree Tilak for helping me with the technical review of the book.

Disclaimer

Although all efforts have been made to ensure the accuracy of the contents of this book, we cannot guarantee 100% correctness of the information contained herein.

If you find any factual anomalies, grammar or spelling errors please send it along with your comments and suggestions to the author.

Trademarks

Overview of Exam

Introduction to ISTQB Agile Foundation Level (CTFL-AT)

This certification is designed for professionals who are working within Agile environments. It is also for professionals who are planning to start implementing Agile methods in the near future or are working within companies that plan to do so. The certification provides an advantage for those who would like to know the required Agile activities, roles, methods, and methodologies specific to their role.

Learning Objectives

The syllabus categorizes learning objectives into three cognitive levels:

- K1: remember, recognize, and recall
- K2: understand, explain, give reasons, compare, classify and summarize
- K3: apply

The relevant learning objectives at K1, K2, and K3 levels are provided at the beginning of each chapter within each particular extension syllabus.

Entry Requirements

To be able to participate in the ISTQB Agile Foundation Level (CTFL-AT), candidates must have obtained the ISTQB Foundation Level certificate.

Exam Structure

This exam is comprised of 40 multiple choice questions. To pass the exam, at least 65% of the questions (26 questions) must be answered correctly.

Content

Chapter 1: Agile Software Development

- The tester should remember the basic concept of Agile software development based on the Agile Manifesto.
- The tester should understand the advantages of the whole-team approach and the benefits of early and frequent feedback.
- The tester should recall Agile software development approaches.
- The tester should be able to write testable user stories in collaboration with developers and business representatives.
- The tester should understand how retrospectives can be used as a mechanism for process improvement in Agile projects.
- The tester should understand the use and purpose of continuous integration.
- The tester should know the differences between iteration and release planning, and how a tester adds value in each of these activities.

Chapter 2: Fundamental Agile Testing Principles, Practices, and Processes

- The tester should be able to describe the differences between testing activities in Agile projects and non-Agile projects.
- The tester should be able to describe how development and testing activities are integrated in Agile projects.
- The tester should be able to describe the role of independent testing in Agile projects.
- The tester should be able to describe the tools and techniques used to communicate the status of testing in an Agile project, including test progress and product quality.
- The tester should be able to describe the process of evolving tests across multiple iterations and explain why test automation is important to manage regression risk in Agile projects.
- The tester should understand the skills (people, domain, and testing) of a tester in an Agile team.
- The tester should be able to understand the role of a tester within an Agile team.

Chapter 3: Agile Testing Methods, Techniques, and Tools

- The tester should be able to recall the concepts of test-driven development, acceptance test-driven development, and behavior-driven development.

- The tester should be able to recall the concepts of the test pyramid.
- The tester should be able to summarize the testing quadrants and their relationships with testing levels and testing types.
- For a given Agile project, the tester should be able to work as a tester in a Scrum team.
- The tester should be able to assess quality risks within an Agile project. • The tester should be able to estimate testing effort based on iteration content and quality risks.
- The tester should be able to interpret relevant information to support testing activities.
- The tester should be able to explain to business stakeholders how to define testable acceptance criteria.
- Given a user story, the tester should be able to write acceptance test-driven development test cases.
- For both functional and non-functional behavior, the tester should be able to write test cases using black box test design techniques based on given user stories.
- The tester should be able to perform exploratory testing to support the testing of an Agile project.
- The tester should be able to recall different tools available to testers according to their purpose and to activities in Agile projects.

1 Agile Software Development

Learning objectives for Agile Software Development

Following learning objectives are covered in this chapter:

1.1 The Fundamentals of Agile Software Development

FA-1.1.1 (K1) Recall the basic concept of Agile software development based on the Agile Manifesto

FA-1.1.2 (K2) Understand the advantages of the whole-team approach

FA-1.1.3 (K2) Understand the benefits of early and frequent feedback

1.2 Aspects of Agile Approaches

FA-1.2.1 (K1) Recall Agile software development approaches

FA-1.2.2 (K3) Write testable user stories in collaboration with developers and business representatives

FA-1.2.3 (K2) Understand how retrospectives can be used as a mechanism for process improvement in Agile projects

FA-1.2.4 (K2) Understand the use and purpose of continuous integration

FA-1.2.5 (K1) Know the differences between iteration and release planning, and how a tester adds value in each of these activities

1.1 The Fundamentals of Agile Software Development

Testers in the Agile project require the same capabilities and skills as those working in the traditional linear development approaches such as waterfall and V-model. However, those capabilities are employed at different times and to different degrees in the context of Agile software development.

To contribute value to Agile software development, testers must understand and reflect the philosophy that underpins Agile work. This philosophy is encapsulated in the Agile Manifesto and accompanying 12 principles.

In Agile, testers are an integral part of a whole-team approach together with developers and business representatives. The team members in the Agile project communicate with each other early and frequently, which helps them remove defects early and develop a quality product.

1.1.1 Agile Software Development and the Agile Manifesto

In 2001, a group of individuals, representing the most widely used lightweight software development methodologies, came across to discuss their work and look for any common themes in their various approaches. By the end of their time, they agreed on a common set of values and principles which became the Manifesto for Agile Software Development or the Agile Manifesto [http://agilemanifesto.org/]

The Agile Manifesto which provides a cornerstone for all Agile methods contains four statements of values:

- Individuals and interactions **OVER** processes and tools
- Working software **OVER** comprehensive documentation
- Customer collaboration **OVER** contract negotiation
- Responding to change **OVER** following a plan

Individual and interactions	Over	Process and tools
Working software	Over	Comprehensive documentation
Customer collaboration	Over	Contract negotiation
Responding to change	Over	Following a plan

The Manifesto of Agile Software Development

The Agile Manifesto does not suggest replacing the items in right with left rather it stresses prioritizing left items over right.

Individuals and Interactions

Agile development argues that there are benefits for the project which use good tools and processes. However, over-reliance on these tools and/or processes subsequently results in rigidity that does not cope up well especially, when there are changes required to the project. As it is the people who produce software, therefore, teams can work most effectively through direct communication and interactions rather than over-relying on tools or processes.

Teams who frequently interact with each other rather than rigidly following the process are proven more effective in software development.

Key exam take-out
• Agile development is people-centered
• The Agile team is composed of small number of team members who possess different skill sets
• The interaction between the team members is close and frequent
• Emphasis is on collaboration among team members rather than rigidly following the processes and over-reliance on tools

Working Software

In Agile development working software with reduced functionality is available much early in the development lifecycle. From a customer perspective, working software is much more useful and valuable than detailed documentation. It gives an opportunity to provide rapid feedback to the development team and can provide business benefits much earlier.

Working software also helps the customers as they are often unsure about what they want until they are able to see a limited working prototype. This approach is especially helpful where the problem areas are new and unclear.

Key exam take-out

- In Agile development, focus is to develop working software regularly and frequently, ideally at the end of each iteration.
- Working system is more useful for the customers than detailed documentation and enables them to provide quick feedback to the development team
- Agile development can confer significant time-to-market advantage due to working software available early
- Working software is helpful where the customer is not clear about the solutions and problem areas
- It helps in bringing innovation in new problem domains

Customer Collaboration

In traditional approaches, as soon as the requirements and scope of the project are confirmed with the customer, contracts are formed, and the team follows that for software development delivery. During the initial phase customers often find great difficulty in specifying system requirements and then in the later phase they are subjected to negotiating the contracts.

Collaborating directly with the customer improves the likelihood of understanding exactly what the customer requires and results in customer satisfaction. Having contracts with customers may be important but having regular and close collaboration with them is likely to bring more success to the project.

Key exam take-out
• Customers may find it difficult to describe the requirements for a system during initial stages
• Collaborating directly with the customer helps to understand the expectations correctly and increases the success of the project
• In Agile development contracts with customers are not set in the center of attention

Responding to Change

The environment in which the business operates such as legislation, competitor activity, technology advances, and other factors can have major influences on the project. To simply ignore this and produce a detailed rigid plan in the early stages of project development is not so useful.

If change is enviable, then it is better to accept the fact and create processes that cope well with change. Agile accommodates these factors in the development process and encourage planning based on the level of detail that is currently available. It encourages flexibility in work practices to embrace change rather than adhering rigidly to a plan.

Key exam take-out
• Software projects are subject to change due to internal and external changes
• Changes have a strong impact on the project and the development process should quickly respond to these changes
• Rigid processes which are unable to accept changes in plans are not useful
• Agile teams are expected to anticipate and welcome change throughout the life cycle

Agile Principles

The core Agile Manifesto values are captured in twelve principles, they are:

1. Our highest priority is to satisfy the customer through early and continuous delivery of valuable software.
2. Welcome changing requirements, even late in development. Agile processes harness change for the customer's competitive advantage.
3. Deliver working software frequently, at intervals of between a few weeks to a few months, with a preference to the shorter timescale.

4. Business people and developers must work together daily throughout the project.
5. Build projects around motivated individuals. Give them the environment and support they need and trust them to get the job done.
6. The most efficient and effective method of conveying information to and within a development team is face-to-face conversation.
7. Working software is the primary measure of progress.
8. Agile processes promote sustainable development. The sponsors, developers, and users should be able to maintain a constant pace indefinitely.
9. Continuous attention to technical excellence and good design enhances agility.
10. Simplicity—the art of maximizing the amount of work not done—is essential.
11. The best architectures, requirements, and designs emerge from self-organizing teams.
12. At regular intervals, the team reflects on how to become more effective, then tunes and adjusts its behavior accordingly.

The different Agile approaches provide prescriptive practices to put these values and principles into action.

Key exam take-out

Agile Principles

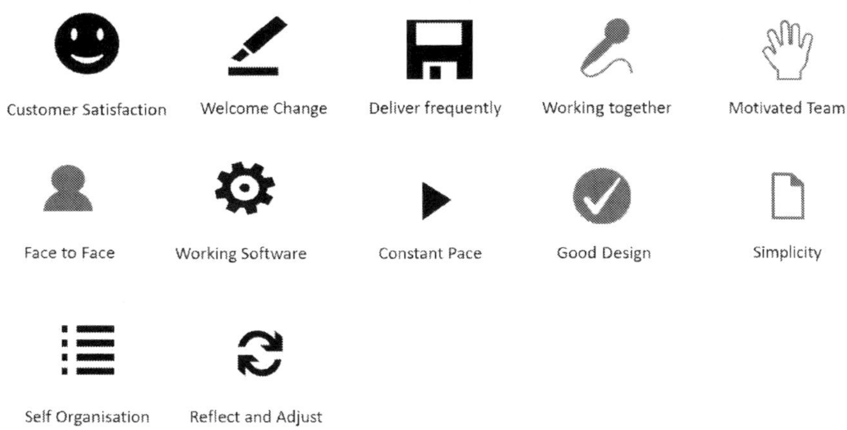

1.1.2 Whole-Team Approach

One of the biggest differences in Agile development versus traditional development is the whole-team approach. In Agile development, the quality of the product is not the sole responsibility of the testers, but it is the responsibility of the whole team. The whole-team approach means involving everyone with the knowledge and skills necessary to ensure the success of the project.

The team includes representatives from the customer and other business stakeholders who help to determine product features. The teams are relatively small with as few as three people and as many as nine people. Ideally, the whole team should share the same workspace, as co-location strongly facilitates communication and interaction.

The whole- team approach is supported through the daily stand-up meetings involving all members of the team, where work progress is communicated and any impediments to progress are highlighted. The whole-team approach promotes more effective and efficient team dynamics.

The essence of the whole-team approach lies in the testers, developers, and the business representatives working together in every step of the development process. Testers work closely with both developers and business representatives to ensure that the desired quality levels are achieved. Testers support and collaborate with business representatives to help them create suitable acceptance tests and work closely with developers to agree on the testing strategy and decide on the test automation approach. Also, testers can help in transferring and extending testing knowledge to other team members and influence the development of the product.

The whole team is involved in any consultations or meetings in which product features are presented, analyzed, or estimated. The concept of involving testers, developers, and business representatives in all feature discussions is known as the **power of three.**

Benefits of the Whole-Team Approach for the Product Development

- Enhancing communication and collaboration within the team
- Taking advantage of the different set of skills for the benefit of the project
- Quality is everyone's objective

Further Benefits of the Whole-Team Approach in Agile Projects

- The whole team is responsible for the quality of the product
- Close collaboration along the complete development process among testers, developers and business representatives

- The whole team takes part in the presentation, analysis and estimation of product features, this involvement is also called "**the power of three**"
- Testers ensure that the desired quality standards are reached by collaborating with:
  - Business representatives for defining suitable acceptance tests
  - Developers for agreeing on the test strategy and automation approaches
  - Other team members for transferring and extending testing knowledge

Key exam take-out
• Involves everyone having the knowledge and skills that are needed to ensure the success of the project
• Includes the testers, developers, and the business representatives and stakeholders who define the project features
• Successful teams are composed of three to nine people
• Communication and interaction can easily take place when the team share the same workspace

1.1.3 Early and Frequent Feedback

In traditional sequential development, the customer is able to see the product quite late as a single finished product is delivered quite late in the development lifecycle. At this point, if there is any customer feedback it is often too late for the development team to address those effectively. Normally, these are dealt as project change requests or additional work requests.

In contrast, Agile projects have short iterations, at the end of each iteration workable software with limited functionality is demonstrated to the customer. This enables the project team to receive early and continuous feedback on product quality.

By getting frequent customer feedback as the project progresses, Agile teams can incorporate most new changes into the product development process. Early and frequent feedback helps the team focus on the features with the highest business value or associated risk, and these are delivered to the customer first.

Early and frequent feedback also helps manage the team better since the capability of the team is transparent to everyone. Agile teams can also use continuous integration to get early feedback on product quality (Section 1.2.4 provides more details on continuous integration).

Key exam take-out
The benefits of early and frequent feedback include: • Avoiding requirements misunderstandings, which may not have been detected until later in the development cycle when they are more expensive to fix • The software is available to the customer early so it can be confirmed that it is fit for the purpose • Helps in finding quality problems early

1.2 Aspects of Agile Approaches

There are a number of Agile approaches but all of them share a common philosophy of collaborative user story creation, retrospectives, continuous integration, and planning for overall release as well as individual iterations.

1.2.1 Agile Software Development Approaches

The different Agile approaches implement the values and principles of the Agile Manifesto in different ways. In this syllabus, three Agile approaches are considered: Extreme Programming (XP), Scrum, and Kanban.

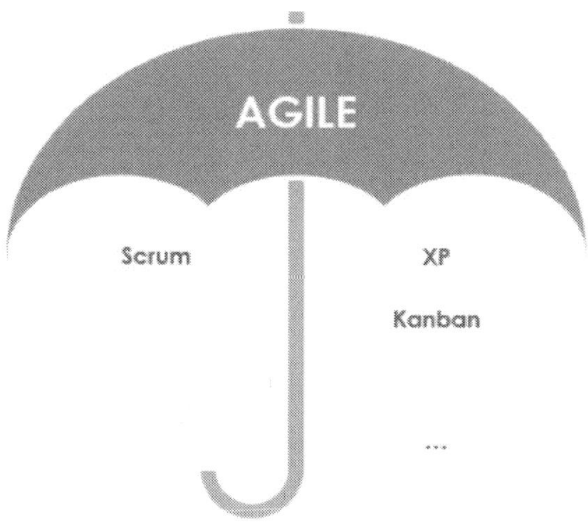

Different Agile Development Approaches

These Agile methods are not mutually exclusive. Extreme Programming (XP) offers an efficient and effective approach to software development. Scrum focuses on the management of the team and process while Kanban is concerned with optimizing the flow of work. Organizations may use a hybrid of any or all of the XP, Scrum and Kanban frameworks.

Extreme Programming (XP)

Extreme Programming (XP) was originally introduced by Kent. In this Agile approach software development is described by certain values, principles, and development practices.

XP embraces five values to guide development:

XP Core Values

1. **Communication**: Everyone is part of the team and the team communicates face to face daily. Team works together on everything from requirements to code. The team creates the best solution to solve any problems.
2. **Simplicity**: Team do what is needed and asked for, but no more. This maximizes the value created for the investment made to date. The team take small simple steps to achieve goal and mitigate failures as they happen.
3. **Feedback**: Team take every iteration commitment seriously by delivering working software. The team demonstrates software early and often then listen carefully and make any changes needed. Team talk about the project and adapt process to it, not the other way around.
4. **Courage**: All the team members tell the truth about progress and estimates. The team doesn't document excuses for failure because they plan to succeed, they don't fear anything because no one works alone. They adapt to changes whenever it happens.
5. **Respect**: Everyone gives and feels the respect they deserve as a valued team member. Everyone contributes value even if it's simply enthusiasm. Developers respect the expertise of the customers and vice versa. Management respects the team's right to accept responsibility and receive authority over our own work.

At a lower level, XP describes a set of 14 principles as additional guidelines:

XP Primary Principles

1. **Humanity**: People develop software. To gain their productivity, support them and provide a rewarding, supportive working environment.
2. **Economics**: The goal is to produce business value not exquisite code or cutting-edge technology.
3. **Mutual benefit**: Look for win-win solutions i.e. the software satisfies all parties.
4. **Self-similarity**: Make an effort to see and understand existing solutions patterns and apply them in new contexts.

5. **Improvement**: There is no perfect process or design – you can always continuously improve. Continuous improvement leads to excellence.
6. **Diversity**: Enhance team productivity through diversity. Bring a a wide array of skills, experience, and perspectives to bear on problems.
7. **Reflection**: Learn lessons from experience.
8. **Flow**: Split larger tasks into manageable chunks to make work-flow more consistently. The uninterrupted work-flow and short iterations keep the project moving.
9. **Opportunity**: Impediments and failures are seen as opportunities. Look for opportunities to learn.
10. **Redundancy**: Avoid repeating steps that can be automated.
11. **Accept failure**: Be prepared to try and fail but view failure as feedback and a chance to learn.
12. **Quality**: High quality increases predictability and efficiency. It is also motivational.
13. **Baby steps**: Many short iterations prompt feedback, fast compensation of failures, and flexibility regarding the framework of the project. Improve in small but frequent steps.
14. **Accepted responsibility**: The team assumes responsibility; no regulations are prescribed by the management.

XP describes **thirteen primary practices**:

1. **Sit together**: Co-located teams communicate more effectively.
2. **Whole-team**: The entire team, with their different skills and perspectives, will produce higher quality outcomes.
3. **Informative workspace**: Visible lists, graphs and notice boards that provide information to assess the current state of progress, current tasks, project status, etc. should be seen from where you are sitting.
4. **Energized work**: An appropriate work/life balance promotes enthusiasm, energy and effective contribution. An atmosphere to work without pressure and no working overtime.
5. **Slack**: Build slack- time into the schedule or include tasks that can be dropped if time is too constrained.
6. **Pair programming**: Two heads are better than one. Promoting self-regulating teams by taking over programming tasks in pairs and alternating partners.
7. **Stories**: Brief statements of required capabilities that, typically represent one or two days of development effort.

8. **Weekly cycle**: Plan weekly. Deciding on a weekly basis, which stories to implement.
9. **Quarterly cycle**: High-level planning (three months) and review of lessons learned, and improvements implemented.
10. **Ten-minute build**: Creating a build (an integrated software version) and executing (automated) tests in a maximum of 10 minutes. Reduces efforts and costs.
11. **Continuous integration**: Integration should last from minutes to a couple of hours to increase efficiency.
12. **Test-first programming** (test-driven development): Tests must be written before the implementation of functionality.
13. **Incremental design**: Incremental design ensures that feedback and insight is incorporated for software improvement

Many of the Agile software development approaches in use today are influenced by XP and its values and principles. Agile teams following Scrum often incorporate XP practices.

Scrum

Scrum is an Agile management framework for managing software development. Scrum terms and concepts, such as sprint and product owner, have become part of the de facto language of Agile. Scrum constituent the following instruments and practices:

1. **Sprint**: Scrum divides a project into iterations, called sprints. Sprints are of fixed length (usually two to four weeks) for the entire project.
2. **Product Increment**: Each sprint results in a potentially releasable/ shippable product (called an increment).
3. **Product Backlog**: The product owner manages a prioritized list of planned product items (called the product backlog). The product backlog evolves from sprint to sprint, this activity is known as backlog refinement.
4. **Sprint Backlog**: At the start of each sprint, the Scrum team selects a set of highest priority items from the product backlog. Collectively, these items will form the sprint backlog. This way of working is based on the "**pull**" principle because the scrum team selects the items from the sprint in contrast to the product owner "**pushing**" items to the team.
5. **Definition of Done**: All functionality or features will have associated acceptance criteria used to verify correctness. However, to be complete and shippable, a piece of software will probably have to satisfy other criteria such as being adequately documented and/or written to an agreed

standard. The Scrum team discusses and defines appropriate criteria for sprint completion.

The discussion creates a deeper level of understanding of the backlog items and product requirements. These discussions help the team to be clear about what constitutes "Done" and deliver a potentially releasable product at each sprint's end.

6. **Time-boxing**: In Scrum time boxing not only fixes the duration of the sprints in a release but also applies to a variety of other activities such as meeting start and end times. Time-boxing sprints mean that only those tasks team believes can be finished within the sprint become the part of the sprint backlog. If the team cannot finish a task within a sprint, the associated product features are moved back into the product backlog.
7. **Transparency**: The development team reports and updates sprint status on a daily basis in a meeting called the **daily scrum**. Interested stakeholders can join the meeting to observe the team progress, also the team task progress is visible on taskboard. This makes the content and progress of the current sprint, including test results, visible to the team, management, and all interested parties.

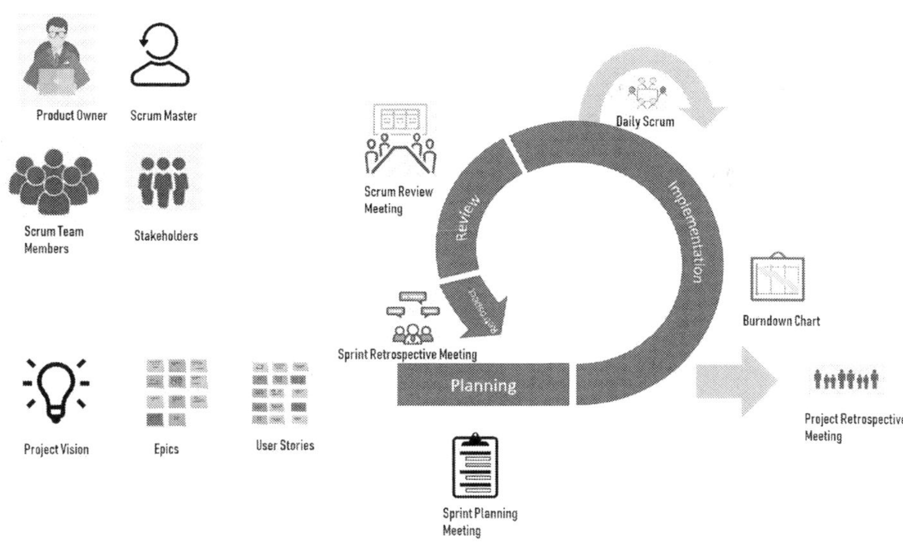

Scrum Lifecycle

Scrum defines three roles:

- **Scrum Master**: Ensures that Scrum practices and rules are implemented and followed and resolves any issues that are impeding team progress and preventing the team from following the practices and rules. Scrum master acts as a coach to the team, not the team leader.
- **Product Owner**: Represents the customer. The product owner creates, maintains, and prioritizes the product backlog. This person is also not the team leader.
- **Development Team**: Develop and test the product.

The team is self-organized and cross-functional. There is no team lead, so the whole team makes the decisions.

Scrum (as opposed to XP) does not dictate specific software development techniques (e.g. test first programming). In addition, Scrum does not provide guidance on how testing should be done in a Scrum project.

Key exam take-out

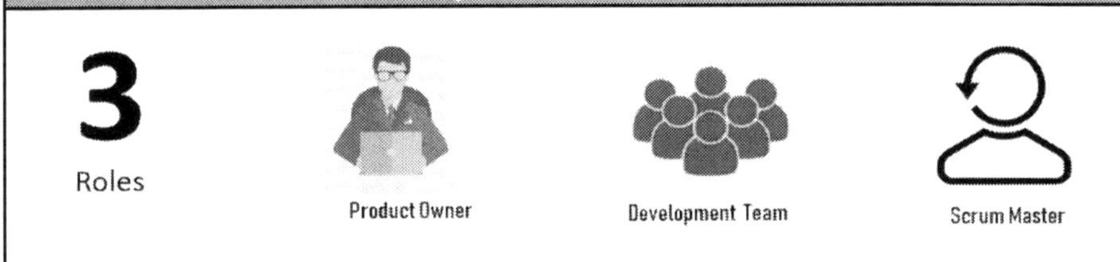

Kanban

Kanban is a Japanese word that means "signal card". It is a process management approach that is often combined with other Agile methods in projects. The general objective is to visualize and optimize the flow of work within a value-added chain. Kanban seeks to make the value-adding process visible so that any problems in the flow of value (bottlenecks, delays, wasting effort, etc) can be seen and addressed.

Kanban utilizes three instruments:

- **Kanban Board**: Kanban board is used to visualize the value chain to be managed. Each column shows a station, which is a set of related activities, e.g. development or testing. The items to be produced or tasks to be completed are symbolized as tickets and are placed in the far-left column of the Kanban board. In this way, the tickets are seen to be part of the backlog. Tickets move from left to right across the board through the stations. Kanban boards are widely used in software development to make the workflow visible.

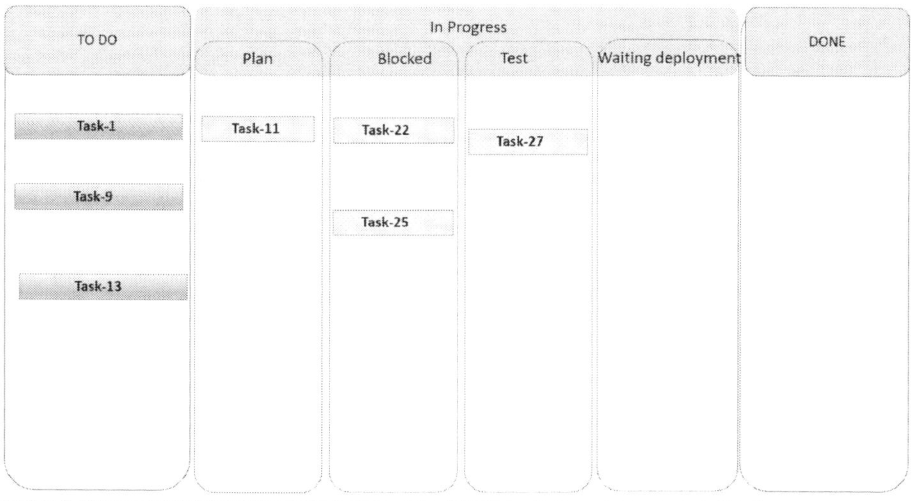

Example of Kanban Board

- **Work-in-Progress Limit**: The amount of parallel active tasks is strictly limited. This is controlled by the maximum number of tickets allowed for a station and/or globally for the board. Whenever a station has the free capacity, the team member pulls a ticket from the predecessor station.
- **Lead Time:** Lead time is the amount of time it takes for a unit of work to travel through the team's workflow–from the moment work starts to the moment it ships. Kanban is used to optimize the continuous flow of tasks by minimizing the (average) lead time for the complete value stream.

Following table display the similarities and differences in Scrum and Kanban.

	Scrum	**Kanban**
Release methodology	At the end of each sprint	Continuous delivery or at the team's discretion
Visualization of tasks	Task boards	Kanban Board
Roles	Product owner, scrum master, development team	No defined roles
Time-boxing (Iterations or sprints)	Mandatory; Shippable product at the end of the sprint	Optional; releasing deliverables item by item
Key metrics	Velocity	Lead time

1.2.2 Collaborative User Story Creation

Traditional requirements specifications are usually created by business analysts and validated by business stakeholders. This approach can result in low-quality specifications as users lack insight into their true needs during the start of the project. The absence of a global vision for the system, redundant or contradictory features, and other miscommunications can further degrade the specifications. Poor specifications are often a major reason for project failure.

In Agile development, user stories are written to capture requirements from the perspectives of developers, testers, and business representatives. **In sequential development**, this shared vision of a feature is accomplished through formal reviews after requirements are written. **In Agile development**, this shared vision is accomplished through frequent informal reviews while the requirements are being written.

User stories most commonly take the following form:

As a <**role**>, I want to <**activity or capability**>

So that <**achieve some valuable outcome**>

Example:

As a **credit card customer**,

I want to **access my monthly repayment record**

So that **I can pay my credit card bill**.

Ron Jefferies proposed the 3C concept to describe the component elements of a user story. The three elements are card, conversation, and confirmation:

- **Card**: The card is the physical media which describes a user story. It identifies the requirement, its criticality, and the acceptance criteria. It also includes expected development and test duration. This card is used in the product backlog, so the description should be accurate.
- **Conversation**: The requirements are communicated and understood, in a number of conversations conducted between the customers, developers and testers. The conversation explains how the software will be used. The conversation can be documented or verbal. The tester perspective adds much to this conversation by asking questions, identifying ambiguity, missing elements such as non-functional aspects and suggesting ways to test the story. The conversation begins during the release-planning phase and continues when the story is scheduled for inclusion in an iteration.

- **Confirmation**: The acceptance criteria, discussed in the conversation, are used to confirm that the story is done. These acceptance criteria may span more than one user story. Positive and negative tests should be used to cover the criteria. To confirm that the story is done, the defined acceptance criteria should be tested and satisfied.

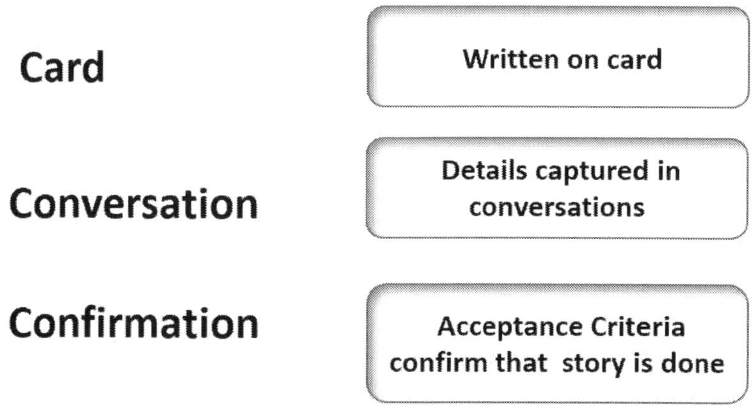

3C Concept

The user stories must address both functional and non-functional characteristics. Each story includes acceptance criteria for these characteristics. These criteria should be defined in collaboration between business representatives, developers, and testers. This provides developers and testers with an extended vision of the feature that business representatives can validate. When a set of acceptance criteria have been satisfied then only the Agile team considers a task as finished. The tester's unique perspective can help to improve the content and quality of user stories by identifying missing details or non-functional requirements. A tester can contribute by asking business representatives **open-ended questions** about the user story, **proposing ways to test the user story**, and **confirming the acceptance criteria**.

The collaborative authorship of the user story can use techniques such as brainstorming and mind mapping. The tester may also use the following **INVEST** technique:

- **I**ndependent: User story is discrete or self-contained, it is not dependent on other user stories. This is particularly important for stories that are being worked on during the same iteration, since dependencies between stories during the same iteration complicate planning and prioritization.
- **N**egotiable: User story is subjected to change based on conversation within the team. The details associated with the story are worked out during this conversation.

- **V**aluable: The user story provides a business value that is clear and readily understood to everyone.
- **E**stimable: The user story needs to be clear enough for the team to be able to do an initial estimate of the story.
- **S**mall: A story has to be small enough to be completed during an iteration.
- **T**estable: The user story has clear acceptance criteria that can be used to create tests to ensure the software is developed correctly.

Agile teams vary in terms of how they document user stories. Regardless of the approach taken to document user stories, documentation should be concise and enough.

Avoiding causes of failure in user stories

- Describe requirements on a shared vision among all people involved
- User stories and acceptance criteria are created in collaboration
- Having informal reviews during the description of requirements
- User stories should address both functional and non-functional characteristics
- Acceptance criteria are defined for each characteristic which helps the developers and testers to understand the expectation of business representatives

Key exam take-out

Tester's role in user story creation

- Help the team in creating user stories by using brainstorming and mind-mapping techniques
- Detect missing details by asking open-ended questions to the business representative
- Identify missing non-functional requirements in stories and help the team to complete them
- Propose different ways to test user stories
- Confirming the acceptance criteria

Exercise:

During the iteration planning meeting, the team is discussing a user story for the new interface which will be integrated to the external applications in later iterations. After the discussion the developers confirmed that they have enough information to start with their development work. The tester suspects there is a gap in requirements as some of the information is missing in the user story which is required for integration testing activities.

What is the BEST choice of action from the tester in this situation?

a) As the Integration testing will be only done after development, the tester can wait and confirm the functionality with the business representatives later.

b) The tester can collaborate with the developers to find out about the missing functionality after the coding is completed.

c) The tester should ask open-ended questions to business representatives to confirm the acceptance criteria and the missing functionality as it may impact the testing activities.

d) The tester should not worry about the gap as it is the team's responsibility to provide all the details to the tester.

Option c) is correct- The tester should make sure that all the information required to complete the testing activities is there in the user story.

1.2.3 Retrospectives

As the name implies, retrospectives are meetings for the Agile teams to look back over a period of work. In Agile development, a retrospective is a meeting to discuss **what was successful**, **what could be improved**, and **how to incorporate the improvements and retain the successes in future** iterations. Retrospectives cover topics such as the process followed, people in the team, organizations, relationships, and tools used or can be used by the team. Regularly conducted retrospective meetings are critical to self-organization and continual improvement of development and testing activities. The success of retrospectives depends on the follow-up activities which occur after the meeting.

Retrospectives may include outcomes that target test-related improvement decisions. These can be focused on test effectiveness, test productivity, test case quality, and team satisfaction. They may also consider aspects such as testability of the applications, user stories, features, or system interfaces. Root cause analysis of defects can drive testing and development improvements.

Retrospectives should be planned at regular intervals. If time-boxed iterations are in use, a retrospective is held at the end of each iteration. Business representatives and the team attend each retrospective as participants while a facilitator organizes and runs the meeting. The team may invite participants from other teams to the retrospective meeting.

Testers play an important role in the retrospectives. Testers are part of the team and bring their unique perspective. Testing activities occurs in each sprint and vitally contributes to success of the project. All team members, testers and non-testers, can provide input on both testing and non-testing activities.

Teams should plan to implement only a few improvements per iteration to allow continuous improvement at a sustained pace. Suggestions for larger changes should be broken down into smaller chunks so that modified ways of working can be introduced over a more realistic longer period.

Retrospectives must occur within a professional environment characterized by mutual trust. The attributes of a successful retrospective are the same as those for any other review as discussed in the ISTQB Foundation Level syllabus.

Results of Retrospective

- Test enhancing decisions are made with respect to
    - Test effectiveness
    - Test productivity
    - Test case quality
    - Team satisfaction
- Decisions are made for improvement of the quality of user stories, code and testing artifacts
- Helps in continuous improvement at a constant speed
- It is a key factor contributing to the team's self-organization capability
- Improvements suggested in Retrospective have an impact on both test and development activities

Timing and organization

- It happens at the end of the iteration
- A moderator/facilitator organizes the meeting and runs it
- The whole team take part in the retrospective which includes business representatives
- The team may invite other persons from another team to participate

Successful retrospective requires

- An atmosphere of mutual trust and respect
- Clearly defined objectives and outcomes with the right attendees
- A positive frame with a focus of improvement
- Issues/problems discussed objectively and welcomed
- A discussion which is not targeted to any team member
- Follow up activities

Key exam take-out

Retrospective

- A team meeting at the end of each iteration to discuss
  - What was successful,
  - What can be improved
  - How to retain successful habits and practices
- Focus is given to the process, participants, organizations and tools
- The goal is continuous improvement and to incorporate improvements in future iterations
- A basic precondition for this meeting is a professional environment & trust among members of the team

Role of the tester

- Testers, as part of the team, play an important part in the retrospective
- Testers bring in their unique perspective to make a substantial contribution to success of retrospective
- Discuss process improvement for both testing and non-testing activities

1.2.4 Continuous Integration

Each increment of product is integrated with the software delivered in preceding increments. This requires reliable, working, integrated software at the end of every sprint. Continuous integration addresses this challenge by merging all changes made to the software and integrating all changed components regularly, **at least once a day**. Configuration management, compilation, software build, deployment, and testing are wrapped into a single, automated, repeatable process. Since developers integrate their work constantly, defects in code are detected more quickly and earlier.

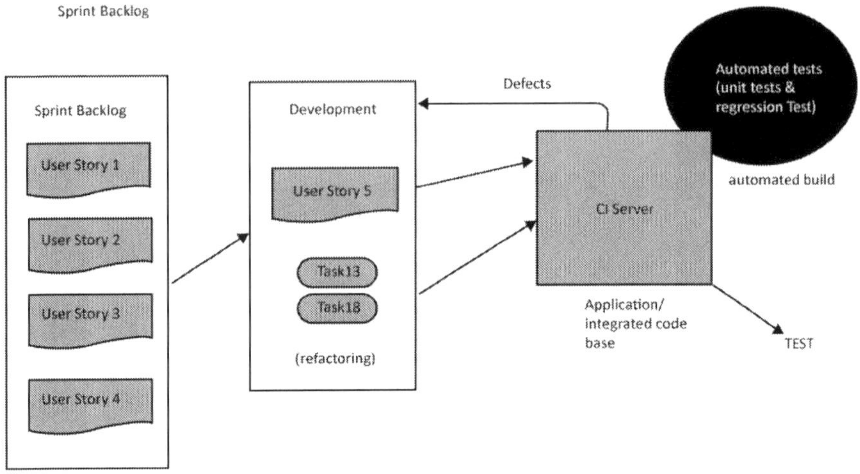

<u>Continuous Integration Process</u>

Following the developers coding, debugging, and check-in of code into a shared source code repository, a continuous integration process consists of the following automated activities:

- **Static code analysis**: The CI server performs static code analysis and report results.
- **Compile**: The code is compiled and linked to generate executables files
- **Unit test**: The CI server executes unit tests, check code coverage and report results.
- **Deploy**: The software build is deployed into a test environment.
- **Integration test**: Integration tests are executed, and the results are reported.
- **Report**: The results of the activities above are posted at a well visible location(dashboard) and/or are sent as a status email to the team.

An automated build and test process take place on a daily basis and detects integration errors early and quickly. Continuous integration allows Agile testers to run automated tests as part of the continuous integration process and get quick feedback on the quality of the code. These test results are visible to all team members when automated reports are integrated into the process. Good automated regression tests cover as much functionality as possible, including user stories delivered in the previous iterations. Good coverage in the automated regression tests helps support building and testing large integrated systems. When the regression testing is automated, the Agile testers are freed to focus on other testing activities.

In addition to running unit and integration tests, CI tools can run additional static and dynamic tests, measure and profile performance, extract and format documentation from the source code, and facilitate manual quality assurance processes. This can result in a significant reduction of time taken to implement continuous quality control.

Build tools linked to automatic deployment tools can fetch the appropriate build from the continuous integration or build server and deploy it into test, staging or production environments. This reduces the errors to install releases in different environments. It also reduces dependencies on team members who are specialized in these tasks and the whole process is more streamlined and quicker.

Continuous Integration in practice

- An automated build and test process take place on a **daily basis**
- Defects and integration errors are found early and quickly
- The team gets fast feedback on the quality of the code
- Quite effective when automated reporting makes these results visible for all team members
- Automated regression tests as part of continuous integration are continuously run during the iteration
- Good regression tests cover as much functionality as possible including user stories of previous iterations
- Manual testing can be intensified on new features, changes and confirmation tests of fixed defects

Risks and challenges

- Introducing the necessary tools and maintenance may take time
- Defining and establishing the processes of continuous integration
- Test automation requires specialists in the team and can be very complex to establish
- Thorough test coverage is essential to achieve the advantages expected from the extra efforts for automated testing
- The tendency to over-rely on unit testing and performing too little integration/system and acceptance testing

CI requires the use of Tools including

- Testing tools
- Tools for automating the build process
- Tools for version control

Key exam take-out
Benefits of properly implemented CI tool
• Earlier detection and easier root cause analysis of integration problems and conflicting changes
• Frequent feedback is provided to the development team on whether the code is working
• Reduces regression risks due to rapid refactoring of the code in Agile projects
• Provides confidence on a solid foundation for every day's work
• Makes progress toward the completion of a product increment visible to developers and testers
• Eliminates the risks associated with scheduling a big-bang integration
• An executable software is constantly available throughout the sprint for testing, demonstration or educational purposes
• Reduction of repetitive manual testing activities so testers get more time to run the exploratory test
• Quick feedback on decisions made for quality improvement and Testing

1.2.5 Release and Iteration Planning

Planning is an on-going activity and is applicable for both traditional and Agile lifecycles.

For Agile lifecycles, two kinds of planning occur:

- o Release planning
- o Iteration planning

Release Planning

Release planning is concerned with the release of the product after the end of the number of iterations or period of time. Release plans are high-level as it happens well ahead of the start of a project and define the product backlog and may involve refining larger user stories into a collection of smaller stories.

In release planning, business representatives in collaboration with the team establish and prioritize the user stories for the release.

Based on these user stories, project and quality risks are identified and high-level effort estimation is performed. Also, project and quality risks are identified which provides the basis for a test approach and test plan for the release spanning all iterations.

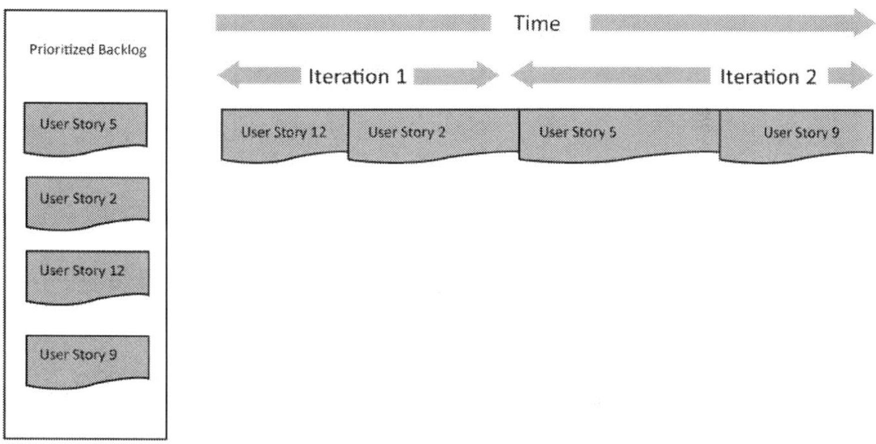

Release Planning

Testers are involved in release planning and especially add value in the following activities:

- Defining testable user stories, including acceptance criteria
- Contributing to project and quality risk analysis
- Estimating testing effort associated with the user stories
- Defining the necessary test levels
- Planning all the testing activities required for the release

Key exam take-out

Following activities are part of Release planning:

- Team members and business representatives work together for the planning activities
- Product Backlog is created
- User stories for the release are defined and prioritized
- Estimation of effort is performed at a high-level
- Test approach and Test plan are defined based on the identified project and product risk

Iteration Planning

Iteration planning is done prior to the start of each iteration. Iteration planning looks ahead only till the end of a single iteration and is concerned with the preparation of the iteration backlog.

In iteration planning, the team selects high priority user stories from the release backlog. These stories are then elaborated, and risk analysis is performed on these user stories. The work required to deliver each story is defined as one or more tasks and estimates are produced.

During the iteration planning meeting, in order to understand the user story, the team may ask clarifying questions to the business representatives and they must provide answers so the team can understand how to develop and test each story.

If a user story is ambiguous and attempts to clarify with business representatives fails, the team can refuse to accept it and select the next high priority story from the backlog.

The number of stories selected is based on established team velocity and the sum of the estimated size of the selected user stories. For example, if the established team velocity is 20 story points then the team can pick four user stories worth five story points each (based on the highest business priority). If there is no exact match the sum of story points can be taken to the nearest velocity. Once the iteration contents are finalized, the user stories are broken into tasks, which are carried out by the appropriate team members.

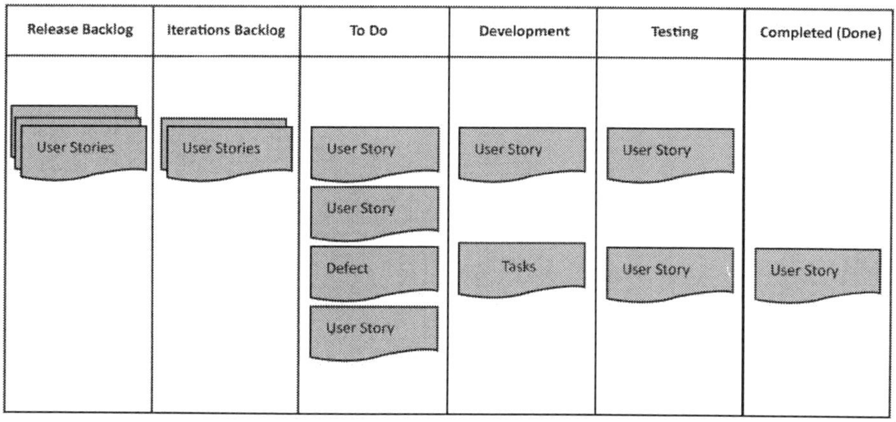

Iteration Planning

Testers are involved in iteration planning and especially add value in the following activities:

- Participating in the detailed risk analysis of user stories
- Determining the testability of the user stories
- Identifying functional and non-functional aspects to be tested
- Creating story acceptance tests
- Creating tasks (particularly testing tasks) for the user stories
- Estimating effort for all testing tasks
- Supporting and participating in test automation at multiple levels of testing

Key exam take-out

Following activities happen during iteration planning:

- The team selects user stories from the prioritized release backlog
- Selected user stories are then elaborated
- Risk analysis is performed on the selected user stories
- Estimation is done for the work-related with each user story
- The team collaborate to understand what is necessary to implement and test each story
- The business representatives help the team to understand the story by providing answers to team questions
- If attempts to clarify a vague user story fail, the team can '**push**' the story back to the backlog and '**pull**' the next high priority story
- After contents of the iteration are agreed, user stories are broken into tasks which are carried out by the appropriate team members
- Velocity (story points per iteration) indicates the productivity of the team and limits the selections of user stories for a particular iteration

Changes are inevitable in Agile projects. These changes may be triggered by internal or external factors. Internal factors include delivery capabilities, velocity, and technical issues. External factors include the discovery of new markets and opportunities, new competitors, or business threats. These factors can change the release plans and may affect the release objectives and/or target dates.

The same is applicable to iteration plans which may change during iteration. For example, a particular user story that was considered relatively simple during estimation might prove more complex than expected.

Such changes can be challenging for testers. Testers must understand the "big picture" of the release for test planning purposes, and they must have an adequate test basis and test oracle in each iteration for the purpose of test development which is discussed in the Foundation Level syllabus. While the required information must be available to the tester early, changes must also be embraced as demanded by Agile principles. This is a dilemma that requires careful decisions about test strategies and test documentation.

Release and iteration planning should address test planning as well as development planning. Particular test-related issues to address include:

- The scope of testing, the extent of testing for those areas in scope, the test goals, and rationale for these decisions.
- The team members who will carry out the test activities.
- The test environment and test data needed, when they are needed, and whether any additions or changes to the test environment and/or data will occur prior to or during the project.
- The timing, sequencing, dependencies (including how the test activities relate to and depend on development activities) and prerequisites for the functional and non-functional test activities.
- Examples include how frequently to run regression tests; which features are dependent on other features or any other test data dependencies.
- The project and quality risks to be addressed (more details of quality risk in Section 3.2.1).
- The team estimation efforts for user stories include time and effort needed to complete the required testing activities.

Key exam take-out
• Release planning is concerned with the planning for the release of the entire product whereas, iteration planning is concerned with the planning for the current iteration.
• Changes can affect both the release and iteration planning.

1.3 Relevant glossary terms and keywords

Glossary term	Definition
Agile Manifesto	A statement on the values that underpin Agile software development. The values are: individuals and interactions over processes and tools, working software over comprehensive documentation, customer collaboration over contract negotiation, responding to change over following a plan.
Agile software development	A group of software development methodologies based on iterative incremental development, where requirements and solutions evolve through collaboration between self-organizing cross-functional teams.
Incremental development model	A type of software development lifecycle model in which the component or system is developed through a series of increments.
Iterative development model	A type of software development lifecycle model in which the component or system is developed through a series of repeated cycles.
Software lifecycle	The use of software to perform or support test activities, e.g., test management, test design, test execution and results checking.
Test Automation	The use of software to perform or support test activities, e.g., test management, test design, test execution and results checking.
Test basis	The body of knowledge used as the basis for test analysis and design.
Test-driven development	A way of developing software where the test cases are developed, and often automated, before the software is developed to run those test cases.
Test oracle	A source to determine an expected result to compare with the actual result of the system under test.
User story	A user or business requirement consisting of one sentence expressed in the everyday or business language, which is capturing the functionality a user needs, the reason behind it, any non-functional criteria, and also including acceptance criteria.

1.4 Summary

Agile software development and the Agile Manifesto: is about

- People and interaction
- Working software
- Collaboration with the customers
- Responding to change
- Twelve principles

Whole-team approach

- Promotes communication in the team
- Making use of different skills for project success
- Quality is everyone's responsibility

Early and frequent feedback

- Avoiding requirement misunderstanding
- Customer expectations are constantly monitored and can be responded
- Finding and isolating quality problems early
- Team productivity(velocity) is transparent and consistent

Agile software development approaches

- Popular Agile development approaches are XP, Scrum, and Kanban
- **XP**: five values, 14 principles, 13 primary practices, Pair programming, Test-First Programming
- **Scrum**: Agile management framework, short iterations fixed duration (sprint)
- **Kanban**: management practice, three instruments -Kanban board, work-in-progress limit, lead time

Collaborative creation of user stories

- **3C concept-** Card, conversation, confirmation
- **INVEST-criteria**: independent, negotiable, valuable, estimable, small, testable
- Testers contribution is important in user story creation

Retrospectives

- End of the iteration meeting for process improvement
- Evaluation of what can be improved, what was successful and how to retain success

Continuous integration

- Static code analysis, compilation, unit testing, deployment, integration/ system test, reporting (dashboard)

Release planning and iteration planning

- **Release plan**: planning for the entire product release
- **Iteration plan**: planning for the current iteration
- Changes can affect both release and iteration plans

1.5 Quiz

Question 1

Which of the following statement best describes the reason for having retrospectives?

Answer:

A. It provides an opportunity for the new team members to learn Agile practice from experienced Agile practitioners.

B. It provides an opportunity to find high-performing team members so they can be utilized for critical tasks.

C. It provides an opportunity for the team to reflect on their success and failures.

D. It provides an opportunity for the team to reflect on their progress and plan for future iterations.

Question 2

Which of the following is NOT a benefit of the Continuous Integration process?

Answer:

A. The team gets fast feedback on the quality of the code.

B. It takes less effort to find the root cause of a defect.

C. Testers test the code which is maximum one day behind code used by developers.

D. The software produced is regularly meeting the business requirement.

Question 3

A tester is involved in which of the following TWO activities during the release planning?

Answer:

A. Defining the test levels

B. Creating acceptance tests for user stories

C. Estimate high-level testing effort for all stories

D. Supporting test automation

Question 4

Which of the following is NOT an Agile Manifesto statement of values?

Answer:

A. Processes and tools over Individuals and interactions
B. Responding to change over following a plan
C. Customer collaboration over Contract negotiation
D. Working software over Comprehensive documentation

Question 5

Match the Agile Manifesto statements (1-4) with their benefits (i-iv) below.

Agile Manifesto statement

1. Responding to change
2. Customer collaboration
3. Individuals and interactions
4. Working software

Benefits

i. It helps in effective interaction and communication.
ii. The team can better understand what the customer wants.
iii. It is more useful for the customers than detailed documentation.
iv. The developed product is more adaptable in the changing environment.

Answer:

A. 1 – iii, 2 – iv, 3 – ii, 4 – i
B. 1 – iii, 2 – ii, 3 – i, 4 – iv
C. 1 – iv, 2 – ii, 3 – i, 4 – iii
D. 1 – ii, 2 – iii, 3 – iv, 4 – i

Question 6

Which of the following is a benefit of the whole-team approach in Agile projects?

Answer:

A. In Agile projects, all team members are required to make any team decisions.

B. In Agile projects, all team members have equal voice irrespective of their roles.

C. In Agile projects, all team members have collective responsibility for quality.

D. In Agile projects, specialized testers are not required.

Question 7

Which of the following practices help to support the whole team approach?

Select TWO options.

Answer:

A. Co-location

B. Test first programming

C. Daily stand-up meeting

D. Continuous integration

Question 8

In Agile projects, early feedback results in which of the following benefit?

A. It helps the team deliver consistent velocity.

B. It helps to deliver better quality software to the customer.

C. It helps to reduce the changes to the software.

D. It reduces the cost of the overall development cycle.

Question 9

Match the following Agile software development (1-3) with the related term (i-iii) on the bottom.

1. Scrum
2. Extreme Programming (XP)
3. Kanban

i. Ten-minute build
ii. Stations
iii. Definition of Done

Answer:

A. 1-i, 2-ii, 3-iii
B. 1-ii, 2-iii, 3-i
C. 1-i, 2-iii, 3-ii
D. 1-iii, 2-i, 3-ii

Question 10

Who plays the 'role' of the team lead in projects following Scrum development approach?

Answer:

A. Scrum Master
B. Product Owner
C. Development Lead
D. None of the above

Question 11

Which of the following are True with respect to tester's contribution during collaborative user story creation?

i. Tester proposing new ways to test the user story.

ii. Tester pointing out that the acceptance criteria are not testable.

iii. Tester asking open-ended question regarding the missing information in the user story.

iv. Tester advising that the business priority of the user story should be changed.

Answer:

A. i, ii, iii

B. ii, iii, iv

C. ii, iii

D. All of the above

1.6 Answers

1	2	3	4	5	6	7	8	9	10	11
C	D	A, C	A	C	C	A, C	A	D	D	A

Question 1

FA-1.2.3 (K2) Understand how retrospectives can be used as a mechanism for process improvement in Agile projects

Justification:

A. Incorrect – This is not the purpose of retrospective.

B. Incorrect – The retrospective meeting is not meant to criticize or reward any individuals or groups.

C. **Correct** –This is the main reason to have retrospectives so the team can reflect on their success and failures and can learn and improve for them.

D. Incorrect – This is not the purpose of retrospective.

Question 2

FA-1.2.4 (K2) Understand the use and purpose of continuous integration

Justification:

A. Incorrect - This is true. The result of the automated test which is part of the continuous integration process gives team quick feedback on the quality of the code.

B. Incorrect - This is true. The new code added which has caused the build to fail is the root cause of a defect, so it is easy to debug and fix the defect.

C. Incorrect - This is true. In continuous integration environment, automated build and test process takes place on a daily basis so the testers are at max one day behind the developers.

D. **Correct**– This is false. Acceptance testing is required to prove the software produced is meeting the business requirement.

Question 3

FA-1.2.5 (K1) know the differences between iteration and release planning, and how a tester adds value to each activity

Justification:

A. **Correct** – This is expected during release planning.

B. Incorrect – This is expected during iteration planning.

C. **Correct** – This is expected during release planning. During the iteration planning, the tester is involved in the estimation of user stories included in the iteration.

D. Incorrect – This is expected during iteration planning.

Question 4

FA-1.1.1 (K1) Recall the basic concept of Agile software development based on the

Agile Manifesto

Justification:

A. **Correct** – False - The Manifesto consists of 4 key values: Individuals and interactions over processes and tools; Working software over comprehensive documentation; Customer collaboration over contract negotiation; Responding to change over following a plan.

B. Incorrect – True – see (A) for the correct answer.

C. Incorrect – True – see (A) for the correct answer.

D. Incorrect – True – see (A) for the correct answer.

Question 5

FA-1.1.1 (K1) Recall the basic concept of Agile software development based on the Agile Manifesto

Justification:

- Project teams that can respond to changes quickly can develop a product that is relevant in the changing environment.
- Close customer collaboration will ensure the team better understand the customer's requirements.
- As Agile development is people-centered through continuous communication and interactions between the individuals, the team can work most effectively.
- From the customer's perspective, working software is more valuable than detailed documentation. It provides an opportunity to give the development team rapid feedback.

Thus:

A. Incorrect.

B. Incorrect.

C. **Correct**.

D. Incorrect.

Question 6

FA-1.1.2 (K2) Understand the advantages of the whole-team approach

Justification:

A. Incorrect – This is not true; all the team members are not always required for team decisions.

B. Incorrect – This is true, but this is not the advantage of the whole team approach.

C. **Correct** – This is true; the main advantage of whole team approach is that the entire team is responsible for quality.

D. Incorrect – This is false, specialized testers (security testers, etc.) are still needed on Agile projects.

Question 7

FA-1.1.2 (K2) Understand the advantages of the whole-team approach

Justification:

A. **Correct** – Co-location supports the whole team approach as it strongly facilitates communication and interaction.

B. Incorrect – Test first programming is not related to the whole team approach.

C. **Correct** – Daily stand-up meeting support whole team approach.

D. Incorrect – Continuous integration provides early feedback, but it is not related to the whole team approach.

Question 8

FA-1.1.3 (K2) Understand the benefits of early and frequent feedback

Justification:

A. **Correct** – Early and frequent feedback promotes consistent project momentum (velocity).

B. Incorrect – Early feedback avoids requirement misunderstanding but not necessarily results in a better quality of software.

C. Incorrect –Due to frequent feedback there may be more changes.

D. Incorrect –This is not always true, as frequent feedback can result in more changes and more testing.

Question 9

FA-1.2.1 (K1) Recall Agile software development approaches

Justification:

A. Incorrect – See (D) for the correct answer.

B. Incorrect – See (D) for the correct answer.

C. Incorrect – See (D) for the correct answer.

D. **Correct** – Definition of Done is used in Scrum to define the appropriate criteria for completion for a particular activity, the ten-minute build is a primary practice in XP, in the kanban board each column is shown as station.

Question 10

FA-1.2.1 (K1) Recall Agile software development approaches

Justification:

A. Incorrect — See (D) for the correct answer.

B. Incorrect – – See (D) for the correct answer.

C. Incorrect – See (D) for the correct answer.

D. **Correct** – There is not Team Lead in the Scrum team. The team is self-organizing and cross-functional.

Question 11

FA-1.2.2 (K3) Write testable user stories in collaboration with developers and business representatives

Justification:

i. This is true. This is important to the user story creation. The tester contributes by ensuring the user story has all non-functional, requirements details.

ii. This is true. This is important to the discussion. The tester contributes by ensuring the team creates testable acceptance criteria for the user story.

iii. This is true. Testers' questions about the missing functionality can result in team discussion about certain complexities of the product being discussed which the team missed earlier.

iv. This is false. This is not part of collaborative use story creation as the business priority of the user story is decided by the product owner or customer representatives.

Thus:

A. **Correct**.

B. Incorrect.

C. Incorrect.

D. Incorrect.

2 Fundamental Agile Testing Principles, Practices, and Processes

Learning Objectives for Fundamental Agile Testing Principles, Practices, and Processes

Following learning objectives are covered in this chapter:

2.1 The Differences between Testing in Traditional and Agile Approaches

FA-2.1.1 (K2) Describe the differences between testing activities in Agile projects and non-Agile projects

FA-2.1.2 (K2) Describe how development and testing activities are integrated in Agile projects

FA-2.1.3 (K2) Describe the role of independent testing in Agile projects

2.2 Status of Testing in Agile Projects

FA-2.2.1 (K2) Describe the tools and techniques used to communicate the status of testing in an Agile project, including test progress and product quality

FA-2.2.2 (K2) Describe the process of evolving tests across multiple iterations and explain why test automation is important to manage regression risk in Agile projects

2.3 Role and Skills of a Tester in an Agile Team

FA-2.3.1 (K2) Understand the skills (people, domain, and testing) of a tester in an Agile team

FA-2.3.2 (K2) Understand the role of a tester within an Agile team

2.1 The Differences between Testing in Traditional and Agile Approaches

The ISTQB foundation level syllabus provides detailed information about the testing tasks related to each development phase. The V- model illustrates this well in context of sequential development methods as shown below in the diagram; user requirements form the basis for the acceptance testing, the functional requirements form the basis for the system tests, technical requirements form the basis for the unit integration tests and program specification form the basis for unit testing.

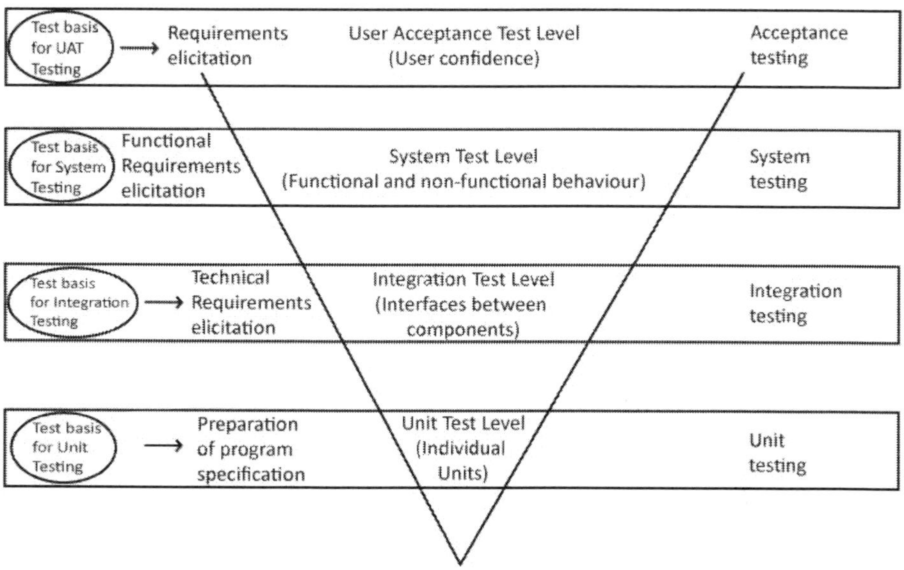

V-model

In the V-model testers are involved from the start of the project, but still, the major part of testing is left till the end when the entire solution is fully developed. A frequent problem associated with this approach is that when the earlier stages overrun, particularly coding, the time remaining for the testing is reduced. As testers get less time to finish the testing it results in a compromise in the earlier agreed testing coverage and quality.

Agile models complete the specification, design, build and test process in small cycles called iteration. Each iteration results in an increment of product which is considered finished only if meets the condition defined in Definition of Done (DOD). There are DODs defined for the release, iteration, feature, each test level, and user story.

Different Agile models differ in terms of how testing and development activities are integrated. Based on the selected Agile model, the project work products, names, entry and exit criteria for various levels of testing, use of tools and how independent testing can be effectively utilized will vary.

Each organization adapts and customizes different Agile practices that are more suitable for them. Therefore, Agile testers should be able to quickly adapt to the context of a given project and the software development practices followed in the project.

2.1.1 Testing and Development Activities

One of the main differences between traditional and Agile lifecycle is the idea of short iterations where each iteration results in working software that delivers features of value to business stakeholders. Release planning is conducted at the start of the project. This is followed by a sequence of iterations. Each iteration in the release begins with an iteration planning session wherein user stories are selected for development, integration, and testing. The development, integration, and testing activities take place throughout each iteration, these activities run in parallel and often overlap each other. Thus, testing activities occur throughout the iteration rather than a final activity.

Testers, developers, and business stakeholders all have a role in testing, as with traditional lifecycles. Developers perform unit tests as they develop features from the user stories and then the testers test those features. Business stakeholders also test the stories before implementation. They may use written test cases but are also likely to explore and experiment with features to provide fast feedback to the development team.

Best practice proposes that no feature is considered done until it has been integrated and tested with the system. In some cases, "**hardening**" or "**stabilization**" iterations occur periodically to resolve any outstanding defects and other forms of technical debt.

Another good practice is to add the defects remaining from the previous iteration to the iteration backlog so they can be addressed first. The problem with this "fix bugs first" approach is that makes it more difficult to know when the total work to be done in the iteration and to estimate when the remaining features can be done.

At the end of the sequence of iterations, there can be a set of release activities to make the product ready for delivery. In some cases, delivery occurs at the end of each iteration.

If risk-based testing is used as one of the test strategies, a high-level risk analysis is done during release planning which is driven by testers. Later during iteration planning the specific quality risks associated with the selected user stories are identified and assessed. This risk analysis highly influences the sequence of development of testing for the features along with priority, estimate and test coverage (Section 3.2 provides more details of risk analysis).

Pairing

Several Agile practices especially Extreme Programming promotes pairing. Initially pairing was conceived as two developers working together on one machine but pairing can also involve two testers working together to test a feature.

Testers can also pair for testing tasks with business representatives and may even work collaboratively with a developer to develop and test a feature. Benefits of pairing include:

- **Increased quality**- Discussion between a pair brings a greater understanding of the issues at hand as well as increased focus on desired outcomes.
- **Spread of knowledge**- Individuals having technical and business domain experience can share knowledge with their partners.
- **Capability uplift**- Less experienced team members can learn from those having more experience.
- **Reduced risk of lost expertise capability**- If one team member leaves the pair or is absent; the other retains the intellectual property and can still move the task forward.

Even where team members are geographically dispersed, pairing is still possible using appropriate tools and procedures.

Product Quality

The whole- team principle makes product quality a team responsibility. This means that everyone must have a fundamental understanding of quality issues and strategies. Testers are well placed to serve as testing and **quality coaches** within the team, sharing testing knowledge and supporting quality assurance work within the team. This promotes a sense of collective ownership of the quality of the product.

Automation

There is an emphasis on test automation at all levels in the Agile based projects. Testers in Agile projects spend considerable time creating, executing, monitoring and maintaining automated tests and results. Developers focus on creating automated unit tests whereas testers focus on creating automated integration, system, and system integration tests. This is a reason that the testers in Agile teams should have strong technical and test automation background.

With the emphasis on test automation in Agile projects, manual testing is likely to focus more on experience-based and defect-based techniques such as software attacks, exploratory testing, and error guessing.

Managing requirement changes

One core Agile principle is that requirement changes can occur throughout the project, changing the existing features have testing implications, particularly around regression testing. Automated testing is one way of managing the amount of test effort associated with these changes. However, it's important that the rate of change does not exceed the project team's ability to deal with the risks associated with those changes. This is also one of the reasons lightweight work product documentation is favored in Agile projects.

Key exam take-out

Agile vs traditional lifecycles

- Short iterations
- Each iteration provides software that has a "business value"
- After the iteration planning, the chosen user stories are developed, integrated and tested
- Development, integration and test activities run in parallel
- As tasks overlap iterations are very dynamic

Stabilization iterations- To resolve lingering defects and other forms of technical debt

"Fix bugs first" approaches - Defects of the previous iteration became part of the iteration backlog and are fixed first before new features are implemented

Key exam take-out

Risks for bug fix first approach

- The total work to be done in the iteration is unknown
- It is difficult to estimate when the remaining features will be finished

Risk-based testing

- A high-level risk analysis is done during release planning
- Testers often are the driving force in risk analysis
- Specific identification and assessment of quality risks takes place during Iteration planning
- Risk analysis influences
    - The sequence of development
    - Priority and depth of testing for features
    - Estimation of test effort required for each feature

Key exam take-out

Pairing

A collaboration of testers and another team member to develop or test a feature

Test- and quality trainer

- Testers act as testing and quality coaches within the team
- Sharing testing knowledge & supporting quality assurance work within a team

Test automation

- Test automation is done for all levels of testing
- Testers spend a lot of time creating, executing, monitoring, and maintaining automated tests and results
- Manual testing on Agile projects is mostly done using experience-based and defect-based techniques
- Developers focus on automating unit tests
- Testers focus on creating automated integration, system, and system integration tests
- Agile teams tend to favour testers with a strong technical and test automation background

Changes may occur throughout the project

- A lightweight work products documentation is more suitable for Agile projects
- Changes to existing features may require lot of regression testing
- Automated testing deals with the amount of test effort associated with changes
- The rate of these changes should not exceed the project team's ability to deal with the associated risks

2.1.2 Project Work Products

In a typical Agile project focus is on delivering working software along with automated tests that demonstrate conformance to requirements therefore vast amounts of documentation is avoided. This applies only to the documentation that does not deliver value to the customer. There is a balance that needs to be found between reduced documentation to increase efficiency and provide sufficient documentation to enable business, testing, development and maintenance activities. During release planning team will decide on the required work products and the level of documentation.

For Agile testers, project work products typically fall into three categories:

1. **Business-oriented work products** that describe the required system (requirements specifications) and how to use it (user guides).

   Typical business-oriented work products on Agile projects include user stories and acceptance criteria. User stories are the Agile form of requirements specifications and explain how the system should behave with respect to a single, coherent feature or function. A user story should define a feature which is small enough to be completed in a single iteration.

   Larger collections of related features, or a collection of sub-features that make up a single complex feature, are widely known as "epics".

   Epics may include user stories for different development teams in the project. The same epic may contain elements of backend and frontend functionality. Each epic and its user stories have associated acceptance criteria.

2. **Development work products** that describe how the system is built (e.g. database entity-relationship diagrams), that actually implement the system (e.g. code), or that evaluate individual pieces of code (e.g. automated unit tests)

   Any technical documents which are prepared before the coding start become part of development work products. Code is the most obvious development work product, but Agile developers often create automated unit tests, which is also a development work product. These unit tests may be created after the code is complete or developers might create tests incrementally before each section of code is started.

3. **Test work products** that describe how the system is tested (e.g. test strategies and plans), that actually test the system (e.g. manual and automated tests), or that present test results (e.g. test dashboards or reports)

Typical tester work products on Agile projects include documents such as test plans, quality risk catalogs etc. which describe how the system is tested, manual and automated tests to actually test the system and test results such as defect reports and tests results logs which provides status of testing. The lightweight approach is used to create all these work products.

In many Agile projects, especially regulated, safety-critical, distributed, or highly complex projects and products, further formalization of these work products is required to satisfy auditors and regulations. Agile uses customer value as the criteria for documentation weight and formality.

Key exam take-out

Business-oriented work products

- User story describing the requirements and how the system will behave
- Epic which are the collections of related features, or a collection of sub-features that make up a single complex feature
- Acceptance criteria associated with each epic and its user stories

Development work products

- Technical documentation
- Code
- Automated unit tests

Test Work products (work product of Agile testers)

- Test strategy, test plans, quality risk catalogue
- Manual and automated tests, defect reports, and test results logs
- Test metrics from defect reports and test results logs

2.1.3 Test Levels

Test levels are test activities that are logically related based on the completeness or maturity of the product under test.

In sequential lifecycle models, the test levels are often defined such that the exit criteria of one level are part of the entry criteria for the next level. Thus, the requirements must be validated and verified during requirement analysis before the solution design begins. Similarly, coded functions must be unit tested before integration testing can take place.

This is not applicable for iterative models where the test levels overlap. Thus, requirement specification, design specification, and development activities often overlap with test levels. This happens because changes to requirements, design, and code can happen at any point in an iteration. Although Scrum does not allow changes to the user stories after iteration planning in practice, such changes sometimes occur.

During iteration, a user story will typically follow the test sequence:

- **Unit testing-** typically done by the developer(s)
- **Feature acceptance testing-** which is sometimes split into two activities:
    - **Feature verification testing-** involves testing against the user story's acceptance criteria. Often automated and may be performed by developers or testers.
    - **Feature validation testing-** involves testing to confirm whether the feature is fit for use. Often manually tested by developers, testers, and business stakeholders working collaboratively. This improves the visibility of the progress and gains real feedback from the business stakeholders.

Regression testing occurs throughout the iteration and frequently runs in parallel with automated unit tests and feature verification tests from the current iteration and previous iterations. Automated regression tests are part of the continuous integration framework.

Some Agile projects have a system test level that starts as soon as the first user story is ready for testing. This involves executing functional tests and non-functional tests (performance, reliability, usability and other test types).

Agile teams can employ various forms of acceptance testing including user, operational, regulatory and contract acceptance tests. For commercial off-the-shelf (COTS) software development internal alpha tests (factory acceptance) and external beta tests (customer site) may also be applicable.

Alpha testing is performed at the developing organization's site, not by the development team, but by potential or existing customers, and/or operators or an independent test team.

Beta testing is performed by potential or existing customers, and/or operators at their own locations. Beta testing may come after alpha testing or may occur without any preceding alpha testing.

One objective of alpha and beta testing is building confidence among potential or existing customers of the system. Another objective is to detect defects related to the conditions and environment(s) if they can't be replicated by the development team.

Acceptance testing is performed at agreed, appropriate points in the development process. This happens likely at the end of each iteration, after the completion of each iteration or after a series of iterations.

Key exam take-out

Test levels:

- **Sequential lifecycle models**- the exit criteria of one level are often part of the entry criteria of the next level
- **Iterative models** -test levels overlap with other test levels or with requirements, design and development activities

Agile Test levels:

- **Unit testing**: Typically done by a developer
- **Feature acceptance testing** is split into
  - **Verification testing**: Often automate; testing against the user stories acceptance criteria by developer or tester
  - **Validation testing**: Manual; developer, tester and business stakeholders work together to check if it is fit for use

Regression testing

- Occurs throughout the iteration
- Runs in parallel with automated unit tests and feature verification tests

System test level

- Starts when the first user story is ready for the test
- Involves functional and non-functional tests

Acceptance tests

- Takes places at close or after the completion of each iteration or after a series of iterations
- Can include user, operational, regulatory and contract acceptance tests
- Alpha and beta tests can also be done based on the product

2.1.4 Testing and Configuration Management

In Agile projects, there is heavy use of automated tools to develop, test, and manage software development. Developers use tools for static analysis, unit testing and code coverage. Developers continuously check the code and unit tests into a configuration management system using automated build and test frameworks. These frameworks allow the continuous integration of new code with the existing one. As soon as the new code is checked-in, static analysis and unit tests are automatically run to verify the new build.

These automated tests can also include functional tests at the integration and system levels. These functional automated tests are integrated with the automated tests run and become part of the continuous integration framework. Depending on the time to run these functional tests they may be separated from the unit tests. For example, unit tests may be run each time new software is checked in, while the longer functional tests are run only every few days.

As multiple developer's check-in the code if any automated test fails during the check-in of new code the team should fix the underlying defects first. This can be achieved if there is real-time test reporting to provide visibility of these build failures to the team. Defects that cause build failure can be detected and fixed quickly in this case since it's easy to find out which new lines of code are checked-in. This approach helps reduce expensive and inefficient test cycles when the whole build is rejected, and the team has to quickly debug the issues and rebuild it again.

Over-reliance on automated unit testing alone to manage regression risks associated with frequent changes can also be a problem. As unit testing often has limited defect detection effectiveness therefore automated tests at the integration and system levels are also required.

Key exam take-out
• New code and automated tests are managed by a configuration management system • Functional automated tests which take a long time to execute are not always run for each code check-in • Defects found during new code check-in should be fixed before the next code check-in • Automated tests at the levels of integration and system are required for better defect detection

2.1.5 Organizational Options for Independent Testing

As discussed in the Foundation Level syllabus independent testers tend to find more defects in comparison to non-independent testers. In some Agile teams, one or more testers may be embedded within the team to perform many of the testing tasks. As Agile teams have collective responsibility for product quality, there is a significant risk that objectivity will be compromised because the testers are "too close" to the development team and form an unconscious bias.

Some organizations have separate, independent test teams that provide testing service during the final days of each sprint. While this preserves independence, time pressures, lack of familiarities with new features and distant relationship issues with business stakeholders and developers may cause problems that impact deadlines and costs.

An alternative, the third option is to create an independent, separate test team and assign testers for the duration of the project. This approach seeks to encourage an independent mindset while providing the longevity of engagement necessary to build beneficial relationships within the team as well as a sound understanding of the product. This independent test team can provide specialized services that are team and/or iteration independent. These include:

- Automated test tools implementation
- Non-functional testing
- Creating and supporting the test environment
- Identifying test data, data cleansing, and maintenance
- Completing test levels (such as system integration testing) that may not fit well within a sprint

Key exam take-out
• To increase independence testers can be assigned for final days of the sprint or on a long-term basis • Independent testers can be used to for iteration-independent activities such as automated test tools implementation, non-functional tests, preparation and set-up of test data/environment, and completing test levels that might not fit well within a sprint

2.2 Status of Testing in Agile Projects

In Agile projects, test status, test progress, and product quality change frequently due to frequent changes. Therefore, it is necessary that the information should be available to the development team and all other interested parties so that they can make appropriate decisions to stay on track for successful completion of each iteration.

Changes in the iteration can impact functionality and features in the increments that were delivered previously. This means that testers must ensure both manual and automated tests are updated appropriately to minimize regression risk.

2.2.1 Communicating Test Status, Progress, and Product Quality

Agile teams progress by having working software at the end of each iteration. To determine when the team will have working software, they need to monitor the progress of all work items in the iteration and release. Testers in Agile teams utilize various methods to record test progress and status.

These include:

- Test automation results
- Progression of test tasks and stories
- Burndown charts

The tester may use the following to communicate progress and status to the rest of the team:

- Verbally- ad-hoc at stand-up meetings
- Task Boards (or Kanban boards)
- Using Burndown charts
- Wiki dashboards & dashboard-style emails
- Customer survey

Verbal

Ad-hoc status updates happen as a result of co-location and collaboration which are common in the Agile projects. In addition, formally scheduled daily stand-up meetings ensure that everyone is up to date about status.

The daily stand-up meeting includes all members of the Agile team including testers. At this meeting, they communicate their current status to other team members. The agenda for each member is to provide the status of:

- Work completed since the last meeting.
- Work planned for completion by the next meeting.
- Anything that is blocking the progress?

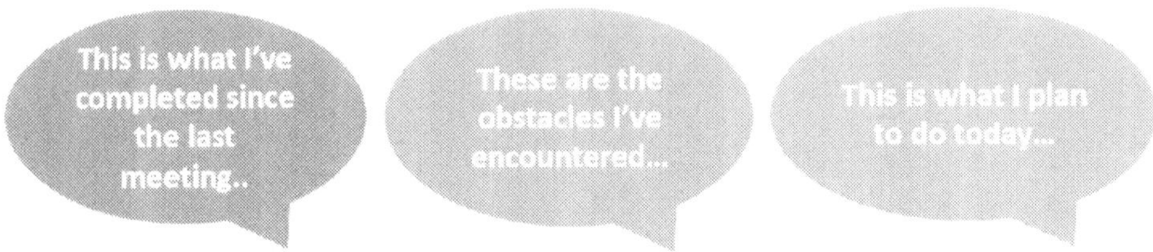

Daily Stand-up Agenda

As issues that block test progress are communicated during the daily stand-up meetings the whole team becomes aware of them and can help the testers in resolving them.

Task Boards

Agile task boards provide an instant, detailed visual representation of the whole team's current status, including the status of testing. The story cards, development tasks, test tasks, and other tasks created during iteration planning are captured on the task board, often using different color cards to easily distinguish the task type.

During the iteration, progress is managed via the movement of these tasks across the task board into columns such as **To do, Work In progress, Verify and Done**. Testing tasks on the task board relate to the acceptance criteria defined for the user stories. As test automation scripts, manual tests, and exploratory tests for a test task achieve a passing status, the task moves into the **Done** column of the task board. The status of tasks on the board is regularly reviewed by the team both ad-hoc and at the daily stand-up meetings. This ensures tasks are moving across the board at an acceptable rate.

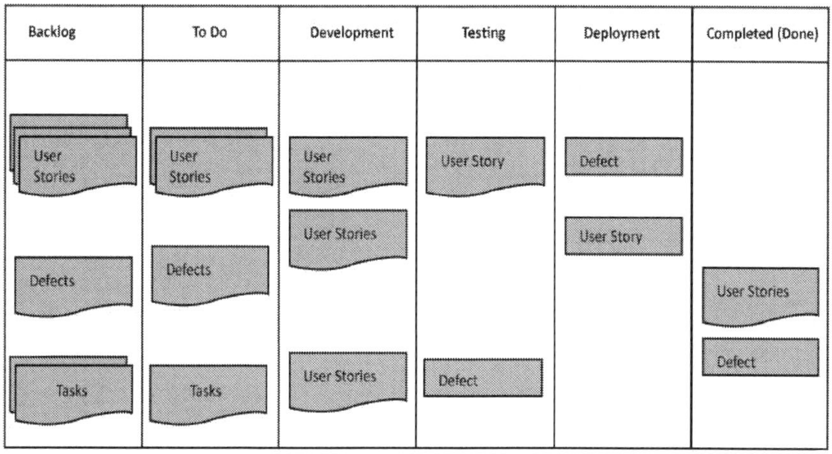

Task board

Burndown Charts

A burndown chart is a graphical representation of outstanding work versus time. The outstanding work is often on the vertical axis, with time along the horizontal. It is useful for predicting when all of the outstanding work will be completed.

Burndown charts are a common way to track progress across the entire release and within each iteration. These charts are simple to maintain, easy to read and show the current state-of-play clearly.

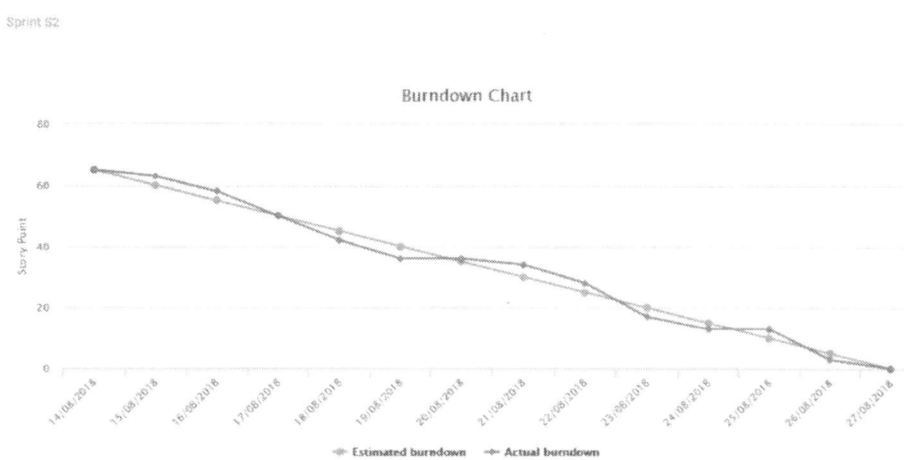

Sprint Burndown Chart

Wiki Dashboards

Agile teams often use software applications to maintain their story cards and Agile task boards. This method of communication also gathers metrics from the testing process, which can be used in process improvement. Communicating test status in such an automated manner also frees testers time to focus on designing and executing more tests.

Agile teams may use tools that automatically generate status reports based on test results and task progress, which in turn update wiki dashboards and send dashboard-style emails to the team.

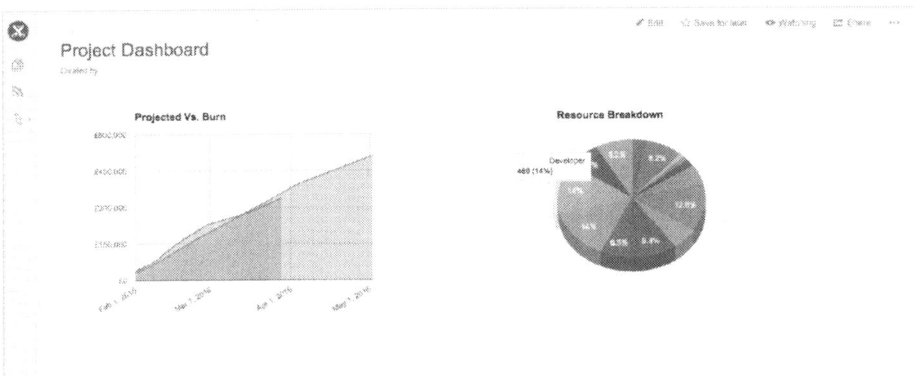

Typical wiki dashboard

Customer survey

Many Agile teams perform customer satisfaction surveys to receive feedback on whether the product meets customer expectations; this information can be used to improve the overall product quality. Traditional development metrics such as test pass/fail rates, defect discovery rates, confirmation, and regression test results, defect density, defects found and fixed, requirements coverage, risk coverage, code coverage, and code churn are also relevant.

As with any lifecycle, the metrics captured and reported should be relevant and aid decision-making. Metrics should not be used to reward, punish or isolate any team members.

Key exam take-out

Ways to communicate test progress:

- **Stand-up meetings** (verbal communication)- Team members communicate their current status, possible problems, and solutions
- **Task Boards** - An instant, detailed visualization of the team's current status including test status
- **Burndown chart**- A visual chart tracking the progress of the product during the project iterations or releases
- **Wiki dashboards**- Automatic update of the status reports & wiki-style dashboards and capability to send dashboard-style emails to all team members and interested parties
- **Customer survey**- Feedback on whether the product meets customer expectations

2.2.2 *Managing Regression Risk with Evolving Manual and Automated Test Cases*

In Agile projects regression risk increases as the scope of testing grows, this may be due to the following reasons:

- Each iteration delivers new functionality which must be tested to ensure it does not adversely affect existing features
- Modifications required by changing business needs and high code churn (lines of code added, modified or deleted from one version to another) may adversely impact features that were developed and tested in previous iterations

It's unlikely that all tests can be repeated in every iteration, therefore, the most appropriate ones should be selected for inclusion in the regression test suite. Testers should regularly review existing test cases (both automated and manual) to identify the right candidate which should be part of the regression test suite and the ones which are no longer part of the suite.

To reduce the required effort, automation is extremely desirable at all test levels and should be done as early as possible. Test automation enables the team to report on **product quality** in a timely manner and well written automated tests provide a living document of system functionality.

It is critical that all test assets such as automated tests, manual test cases, test data, and other testing artifacts are kept up to date with each iteration. The use of configuration management software is very beneficial in this context. Automated tests and test results should be checked-in to the configuration management system along with the associated product build. This means that the team is able to review the functionality and test results for any given build. To avoid software build failures, only code that has passed the automated unit tests should be checked-in.

Automated unit tests are run before source code is checked into the configuration management system to ensure the code changes do not break the software build. To reduce build failures code should not be checked-in unless all automated unit tests are passed. Automated unit test results provide immediate feedback **on code and build quality**, but not on product quality.

Automated acceptance tests are run at least daily as part of the continuous integration full system build. It is not likely that they are run with each code check-in because they take significant time and would slow down iteration progress. The test results from automated acceptance tests provide feedback on **product quality with respect to regression since the last build**, but NOT on status of overall product quality.

The automated regression test suite is also typically run as part of the daily main build in the continuous integration environment. It will be run again when a new build is deployed into the test environment. If the automated regression test fails, the team should stop their current task and investigate the reasons for failure. If the test failure identifies a defect, best practice suggests that it should be fixed before continuing with new coding. Some test fails because they are out of date and don't reflect an agreed change of requirement that has been included in the current iteration. Alternatively, the test may need to be retired if another test has been built to cover the changes.

A build verification test (BVT) is a subset of automated tests to cover critical system functionality and integration points. Results from the build verification tests provide instant feedback on the software after deployment, so teams don't waste time testing an unstable build.

Automation should also be used to support other test activities to give the team more time to develop and test new features. These activities include:

- Generating Test data
- Loading test data into systems
- Deployment of builds into the test environments
- Restoration of a test environment to a baseline
- Comparing data outputs

Key exam take-out

Managing change

- Product grows with each iteration which may affect existing features
- New changes & code churn can impact the previously delivered features

Regression testing

- Due to the tight timeline complete repetition of all tests is seldom possible
- Time should be allocated in each iteration to review manual and automated test cases
- New test cases should be selected that may become part of the regression test suite
- Old test cases which are not relevant should be retired (e.g. due to feature changes)
- Well-written automated tests provide a living document of system functionality
- Good configuration management keep all the test artifacts up to date

Automated unit tests

- Automated unit tests are run before source code is checked-in
- Code should only be checked after all automated unit tests are passed
- Unit test results provide immediate feedback on code and build quality
- Product quality is not the focus of unit tests

Automated acceptance testing

- They are part of the continuous integration full system build
- Run against a complete system build at least daily
- They take longer to run than automated unit tests
- Can slow down the process therefore not run with each code check-in
- Provide feedback on product quality with respect to regression since the last build
- They do not provide a status of overall product quality

Key exam take-out

Build verification tests (BVT)

- There are a minimum set of automated tests that cover critical system functionality and integration points, they are run before a new build is deployed into the test environment
- The results from BVT provide instant feedback on the software after deployment
- An automated BVT can save time of the team in avoiding testing an unstable build

Automated regression testing runs as part of the daily main build

- Run as part of daily main build in the continuous integration environment
- Run again when a new build is deployed into the test environment
- Whenever an automated regression test fails the team stops other activities and investigates the reasons for failure
- The test may have failed due to legitimate functional changes; therefore, the test may need to be updated
- If the test failed due to a defect, it is best practice to fix the defect prior to progressing with new features

2.3 Role and Skills of a Tester in an Agile Team

The role of a tester is to ensure that the software works exactly as it is required and agreed to work. This is true for testers working in traditional and Agile projects. In an Agile team, testers must closely collaborate with all other team members and with business stakeholders. This may have a number of implications in terms of the skills a tester must have and the activities they perform within an Agile team.

2.3.1 Agile Tester Skills

The difference between Agile and traditional testing is broad, a greater emphasis on some skills over others and the time or stage at which various skills are utilized. Agile testers should have all the testers' skills mentioned in the Foundation Level syllabus. In addition to these skills, a tester in an Agile team should be competent in:

- Test automation
- Test-driven development (TDD)
- Acceptance test-driven development (ATDD)
- White-box testing
- Black-box testing
- Experience-based testing.

Testing is continuously changing and evolving with the introduction of new tools and techniques. As Agile methodologies depend heavily on collaboration, communication, and interaction between the team members as well as stakeholders outside the team, testers in an Agile team should have good interpersonal skills.

Testers in Agile teams should be:

- Positive and outcome/solution-driven
- Help the team and other relevant stakeholders to define testable requirements (user stories) with acceptance criteria
- Quality-oriented, skeptical thinking about the product and critically assess the product
- Actively acquire information from stakeholders (rather than relying entirely on written specifications)
- Accurately evaluate and report test results, test progress, and product quality

- Work effectively to define testable user stories, especially acceptance criteria, with customer representatives and stakeholders
- Collaborate within the team, working in pairs with programmers and other team members
- Respond quickly and positively to changes, including modification of test artifacts
- Plan and organize their own work

Testers in Agile teams should also look at continuous skills growth, including personal and interpersonal skills.

2.3.2 The Role of a Tester in an Agile Team

The Agile approach places responsibility for quality on all of the team members so everyone has a role in the test-related effort. In addition to the activities the Agile tester's role is likely to include (collaborative) responsibility for:

- Understanding, implementing and updating the test strategy
- Use of testing tools
- Configure and manage test environments and test data
- Coaching other team members in relevant aspects of testing
- Measuring and reporting test coverage across all applicable coverage dimensions
- Reporting defects and working with the team to resolve them
- Ensuring that appropriate testing tasks are scheduled during release and iteration planning
- Actively collaborating with developers and business stakeholders to clarify requirements, especially in terms of testability, consistency, and completeness
- Participating proactively in team retrospectives, providing feedback on process quality, suggest and implement improvements
- Providing feedback on test status, test progress, and product quality

As testing is not the sole quality mechanism, Agile testers are also concerned with assessing and contributing to development process improvement. This is typically addressed in regularly scheduled retrospectives which are designed to identify and plan for better ways of working.

Agile organizations may encounter some test-related organizational risks:

- Testers working so closely to developers that they lose the objectivity
- Testers become tolerant of or silent about inefficient, ineffective, or low-quality practices within the team due to team relationship
- Testers cannot keep pace with the excessive changes in time-constrained iterations

These risks can be mitigated by using variations of independence testing discussed earlier.

2.4 Relevant glossary terms and keywords

Glossary term	Definition
Build verification test	A set of automated tests which validates the integrity of each new build and verifies its key/core functionality, stability and testability.
Configuration item	An aggregation of work products that are designated for configuration management and treated as a single entity in the configuration management process.
Configuration management	A discipline applying technical and administrative direction and surveillance to identify and document the functional and physical characteristics of a configuration item, control changes to those characteristics, record and report change processing and implementation status, and verify compliance with specified requirements.

2.5 Summary

Testing and development activities

- Short iterations; testers, developers & business stakeholders all have role in testing
- Risk-based testing is done based on risk analysis
- Hardening iterations are used to fix outstanding defects or technical debts
- Pairing involves two team members working together
- Testers as a quality coach for team
- Test automation at all test levels
- Manual tests focused on experience & defect-based techniques
- Lightweight work product documentation

Project work products

- **Business-oriented**: artifacts created by business
- **Development oriented:** artifacts created by developers
- **Test oriented**: artifacts created by testers

Test levels

- Overlapping test levels
- Unit tests (developer), verification test (developer or tester), validation test (developer, tester and business stakeholders)
- Regression testing (automated unit tests and verification tests)
- System test level for functional and non-functional Tests
- Acceptance test level (alpha/beta-acceptance testing, operational, contract, and regulatory acceptance testing)

Testing and configuration management tools

- Code & automated tests are checked-in the configuration management system using automated build and test framework
- Integration and system tests are included in automated tests for better defect detection

Independent Testing

- On-demand testers for final days of sprint
- Testers from test team assigned for the duration of Agile project
- For activities which are iteration-independent and not fit within the sprint

Communicating the status of test activities, progress and product quality

- Use of burndown charts, task board, daily stand-ups for test progress
- Definition and use of appropriate metrics for assessment/evaluation of the product quality (customer satisfaction surveys)

Effectively dealing with the regression risk with evolving manual and automated tests

- Key principle: managing change
- Complete repetition of all tests from the previous iteration is not feasible
- Regular test case review to identify new ones which can be added to the regression suite and the ones which can be excluded from the suite
- Test cases should be kept up to date
- Sensible use of automated unit tests and acceptance testing to manage changes
- Other test tasks may also be automated (generation of test data etc.)

Role and Skills of a Tester in Agile team

Agile tester skills

- In addition to basic testing skills additional skills are needed e.g. test automation, TDD, white-box testing, etc.
- Provide precise results and assessment of test progress
- Positive communication within the team and with stakeholders
- Continuous skills growth in interpersonal skills

Role of a tester in an Agile team

- Determining test status and reporting it, assessment of test progress and product quality
- Identify and implement possible improvement of processes
- Maintain the independence of testing and not lose objectivity

2.6 Quiz

Question 1

Which of the following approach can be used effectively deal with lingering defects and technical debts in Agile projects?

Answer:

A. Having stabilization iterations after every few iterations

B. Heavy use of automation tests.

C. Fixing them after the end of all iterations.

D. Involving business representatives in testing lingering defects.

Question 2

Which of the following is NOT a 'Test work product'?

Answer:

A. Automated tests

B. Test results

C. Database entity diagrams

D. Test plan

Question 3

What is the purpose of feature verification testing?

Answer:

A. To verify the user story against the acceptance criteria

B. To get feedback from the business stakeholders

C. To verify the non-functional attribute of the user story

D. To get feedback on product quality

Question 4

As automated unit test has limited defect detection effectiveness, which of the following can be used to increase the effectiveness of automation tests to reduce regression risks?

Answer:

A. Running the automated unit test suite at least once in a day
B. Using a Test-driven development
C. Including automation tests at the integration and system levels
D. Using a configuration management system

Question 5

Which of the following test activity is NOT performed during the iteration?

Answer:

A. Identification of quality risks
B. Unit testing
C. Feature verification testing
D. Feature validation testing

Question 6

The test manager has observed that the testing team members are working so closely with the developers that they have lost the testers' mindset and testing objective. The recommendation is to separate the testing team from development team and provide testing as a service at the end of the iteration. This approach can introduce which of the following risk? Select the BEST option.

Answer:

A. This will result in a lack of understanding of the feature and relationship issue which will result in increased testing effort.
B. There is no risk as this approach will bring independence and objective evaluation.
C. This may increase regression risk as the testers are not involved from the start of the iteration.
D. This may impact the test estimates as the development team may not be able to estimate the testing tasks correctly in absence of testers during iteration planning.

Question 7

What is the BEST reason to perform customer satisfaction surveys in Agile projects?

Answer:

A. To track progress across the entire release

B. To find out blockers for project

C. To get the latest team status

D. To know overall product quality

Question 8

The team is looking for a way to show the stakeholders' current development progress against the planned development. Which of the following is BEST suited for this purpose?

Answer:

A. Burndown charts

B. Team status report

C. Inviting stakeholders to daily stand up meetings

D. Agile task boards

Question 9

Why is regression risk greater in the Agile development project as compared to traditional development projects? Select TWO options.

Answer:

A. Changes to previously delivered features to meet business can impact the existing functionality.

B. There are few testers in the Agile project as compared to traditions projects to test the features.

C. In Agile development, there is high code churn due to business needs and refactoring.

D. Due to the high speed of development, all the features can't be tested.

Question 10

Why is Test automation important in Agile projects? Select TWO options.

Answer:

A. It can help to reduce regression risk due to frequent code changes.

B. It ensures that all previously delivered features are tested.

C. It provides immediate feedback on overall product quality.

D. It gives testers more time to focus on testing current iteration user stories.

Question 11

For better productivity test team should plan to automate which of the following tasks?

i. Comparison of flat database files due to database upgrade

ii. Restoring the test environment to baseline after the batch program failed

iii. Creation of test data for performance testing

iv. Masking and loading the test data from production to test environment

Answer:

A. i, ii, iii

B. i, ii, iv

C. ii, iii, iv

D. All of the above

Question 12

Which of the following are Agile Tester skills?

i. Able to perform experience-based testing

ii. Able to do test automation

iii. Able to pair with developers to write code

iv. Able to collaborate with other team members

Answer:

A. i, ii, iv

B. i, ii, iii

C. ii, iii, iv

D. All of the above

Question 13

For a new project, the Agile team is seeking new testers. Experience in which of the following tasks will be ideal for a tester to perform their tasks efficiently?

i. Creation and implementation of the test strategy.

ii. Measuring and reporting test coverage for all test levels.

iii. Preparation of burndown chart for entire release and all iterations.

iv. Configuration and management of test data.

Answer:

A. i, ii, iii

B. i, ii, iv

C. ii, iii, iv

D. All of the above

Question 14

Which of the following is a test related organization risk that organizations following Agile methodology may encounter?

Answer:

A. Testers cannot keep pace with the frequent changes in the iterations.

B. Testers coaching other team members in the relevant aspects of testing.

C. Testers suggesting and implementing process improvements.

D. Testers helping the other team members for non-testing activities.

2.7 Answers

1	2	3	4	5	6	7	8	9	10	11	12	13	14
A	C	A	C	A	A	D	A	A, C	A, D	D	A	B	A

Question 1

FA-2.1.1 (K2) Describe the differences between testing activities in Agile projects and non-Agile projects

Justification:

A. **Correct** – Hardening or stabilization iterations are used periodically to resolve technical debt and lingering defects in Agile development.

B. Incorrect – Automation test can't resolve technical debt and lingering defects.

C. Incorrect – Technical debts and defects need to be resolved earlier rather than till end of all iterations.

D. Incorrect – It is about resolving the defects not only testing them.

Question 2

FA-2.1.2 (K2) Describe how development and testing activities are integrated in Agile projects

Justification:

A. Incorrect- This is true. Automated tests are Test work products.

B. Incorrect -This is true. Test results are Test work products.

C. **Correct** – This is false. Database entity diagrams are development work products.

D. Incorrect- This is true. A test plan is Test work products.

Question 3

FA-2.1.2 (K2) Describe how development and testing activities are integrated in Agile projects

Justification:

A. **Correct**- Feature verification testing involves testing against the user story acceptance criteria.

B. Incorrect - This is not the purpose of feature validation testing.

C. Incorrect - This is the not the purpose for feature verification testing

D. Incorrect - This is not the purpose of feature verification testing.

Question 4

FA-2.1.2 (K2) Describe how development and testing activities are integrated in Agile projects

Justification:

A. Incorrect - Running the unit test again and again will not increase the effectiveness.

B. Incorrect - TDD is not related to automation test effectiveness to deal with regression risks.

C. **Correct** - Automation test at integration and system levels are required to increase and effectiveness of automation and reduce regression risk due to frequent changes.

D. Incorrect - Configuration management system is required to manage all the automation test suite and code but is not related to defect detection effectiveness.

Question 5

FA-2.1.2 (K2) Describe how development and testing activities are integrated in Agile projects

Justification:

A. **Correct** - Identification of quality risk is not a test activity performed during iteration. It is done during sprint zero (before start of all iterations)

B. Incorrect - Unit testing is typically done by the developers during iteration.

C. Incorrect - Feature verification testing which is often automated is typically done by the developers or testers during iteration.

D. Incorrect -Feature validation testing which is usually manual and is typically done by the developers, testers and business stakeholders during iteration.

Question 6

FA-2.1.3 (K2) Describe the role of independent testing in Agile projects

Justification:

A. **Correct** – Testers in Agile teams are required to participate in all the activities from the start of the iteration.

B. Incorrect – There is a risk associated with this approach of independent testing.

C. Incorrect – This is not a risk with independent testing.

D. Incorrect – This is not a risk with independent testing.

Question 7

FA-2.2.1 (K2) Describe the tools and techniques used to communicate the status of testing in an Agile project, including test progress and product quality

Justification:

A. Incorrect – Burndown charts are used to track the progress across the entire release.

B. Incorrect – Blockers are communicated in daily Stand-up meeting issues so the whole team is aware and help in resolving it.

C. Incorrect – Agile Task boards are used for visual representations of the whole team's current status.

D. **Correct** – Customer satisfaction surveys are used to receive feedback on whether the product meets the customer's expectation (overall product quality).

Question 8

FA-2.2.1 (K2) Describe the tools and techniques used to communicate the status of testing in an Agile project, including test progress and product quality

Justification:

A. **Correct** – Burndown charts are best to show the stakeholders' current development progress against the planned development.

B. Incorrect - Team status report doesn't show the development progress against plan.

C. Incorrect - Daily stand up meeting is helpful to know the team members' current status.

D. Incorrect - Agile Task boards are used for visual representations of the whole team's current status.

Question 9

FA-2.2.2 (K2) Describe the process of evolving tests across multiple iterations and explain why test automation is important to manage regression risk in Agile projects

Justification:

A. **Correct** – This is a reason for the higher risk in the Agile development project.

B. Incorrect – This is not a reason for high regression risk.

C. **Correct** – This is a reason for the higher risk in the Agile development project.

D. Incorrect – This is not a reason for high regression risk.

Question 10

FA-2.2.2 (K2) Describe the process of evolving tests across multiple iterations and explain why test automation is important to manage regression risk in Agile projects

Justification:

A. **Correct**- Test Automation is necessary to reduce the regression risk in Agile projects.

B. Incorrect - It is not feasible to automate and run all of the delivered features tests from all of the previous iteration.

C. Incorrect - Automated acceptance test results can provide feedback on product quality with respect to the regression since the last build, but they do not provide the status of overall product quality.

D. **Correct** - Automation reduces the regression test effort so the team can focus on tasks from the current iteration.

Question 11

FA-2.2.2 (K2) Describe the process of evolving tests across multiple iterations, and explain why test automation is important to manage regression risk in Agile projects

Justification:

A. Incorrect - See Answer (D) for the explanation.

B. Incorrect - See Answer (D) for the explanation.

C. Incorrect - See Answer (D) for the explanation.

D. **Correct** - All of these tasks can be automated to reduce the overhead and allow the team to spend time developing and testing new features.

Question 12

FA-2.3.1 (K2) Understand skills (people, domain and testing) of a tester in an Agile team

Justification:

A. **Correct** – i, ii and iv are Agile tester skills, the tester in Agile projects are not required to write code with the developers.

B. Incorrect – See answer (A) for the explanation.

C. Incorrect – See answer (A) for the explanation.

D. Incorrect – See answer (A) for the explanation.

Question 13

FA-2.3.2 (K2) Understand the role of a tester within an Agile team

Justification:

A. Incorrect – See answer(B) for the explanation.

B. **Correct** – i, ii and iv are required by the testers in the Agile project. Preparing burndown chart is not the task of tester, it is done by Scrum master.

C. Incorrect – See answer(B) for the explanation.

D. Incorrect – See answer(B) for the explanation.

Question 14

FA-2.3.2 (K2) Understand the role of a tester within an Agile team

Justification:

A. **Correct** – Agile organizations may encounter this test related risk.

B. Incorrect – This is not a test related organization risk. This is required from an Agile tester.

C. Incorrect – This is not a test related organization risk. This is required from an Agile tester.

D. Incorrect – This is not a test related organization risk. This is required from an Agile tester.

3 Agile Testing Methods, Techniques, and Tools

Learning objective for Agile Testing Methods, Techniques, and Tools

Following learning objectives are covered in this chapter:

3.1 Agile Testing Methods

FA-3.1.1 (K1) Recall the concepts of test-driven development, acceptance test-driven development, and behavior-driven development

FA-3.1.2 (K1) Recall the concepts of the test pyramid

FA-3.1.3 (K2) Summarize the testing quadrants and their relationships with testing levels and testing types

FA-3.1.4 (K3) For a given Agile project, practice the role of a tester in a Scrum team

3.2 Assessing Quality Risks and Estimating Test Effort

FA-3.2.1 (K3) Assess quality risks within an Agile project

FA-3.2.2 (K3) Estimate testing effort based on iteration content and quality risks

3.3 Techniques in Agile Projects

FA-3.3.1 (K3) Interpret relevant information to support testing activities

FA-3.3.2 (K2) Explain to business stakeholders how to define testable acceptance criteria

FA-3.3.3 (K3) Given a user story, write acceptance test-driven development test cases

FA-3.3.4 (K3) For both functional and non-functional behavior, write test cases using black box test design techniques based on given user stories

FA-3.3.5 (K3) Perform exploratory testing to support the testing of an Agile project

3.4 Tools in Agile Projects

FA-3.4.1 (K1) Recall different tools available to testers according to their purpose and to activities in Agile projects

3.1 Agile Testing Methods

Agile testing methods are not different from traditional testing methods but just the timing of the testing activities is much earlier with the focus to prevent defects as early as possible. These testing practices can be followed by testers in every development project to produce quality products. Agile testers guide the use of following testing practices throughout the lifecycle.

- Creating tests in advance to express proper behavior of the system under test
- Focus on early defect prevention, detection, and remediation
- Running the right type of test at the right time and as part of the right test level

3.1.1 Test-Driven Development, Acceptance Test-Driven Development, and Behavior-Driven Development

Test-Driven Development (TDD), Acceptance Test-Driven Development (ATDD), and Behavior-Driven Development (BDD) are three related techniques to carry out testing across the various test levels in Agile projects. In all of these technique's tests are defined before the code is written which is an example of early testing from Foundation level syllabus.

Test-Driven Development

Test-driven development became popular through Extreme Programming (XP) approach but is also used in other Agile methodologies including sequential lifecycles. It helps developers focus on clearly defined expected results. The tests are automated and are used in continuous integration. Test-driven development (TDD) is used to develop code guided by automated test cases. The process for test-driven development is:

- Create a test that represents the developers' view of an unwritten code element for a particular requirement; add it to any existing tests
- Run the test, which should fail since the code doesn't exist
- Write the code and run the test in a tight loop until the test passes
- Refactor the code (restructure the existing code without changing its external behavior) after the test is passed, re-run the test to ensure it continues to pass against the refactored code
- Repeat this process for the next small piece of code, running the previous tests as well as the added tests

Test passed can be an exit criterion for coding. The tests written are primarily for unit level and are code-focused, though tests may also be written for the integration or system levels.

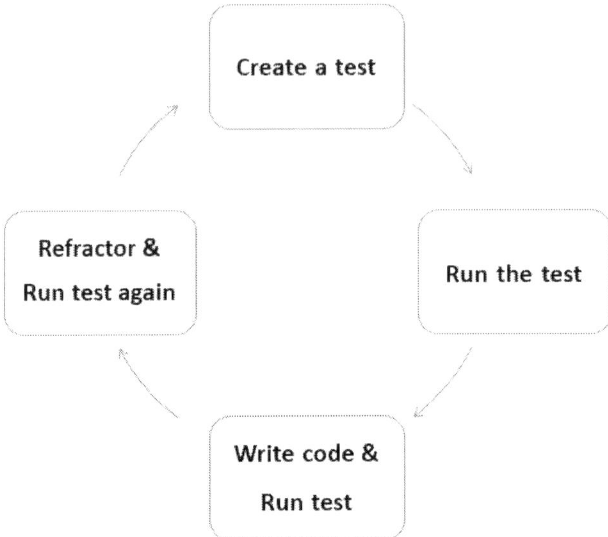

Test-Driven Development Process

Key exam take-out
• Tests are written first and automated then afterward code for the real functionality is written • Tests are primarily at the unit level (component test) • These tests are automated and used in continuous integration • TDD is mainly used in Extreme Programming but can be used in other Agile methodologies and sequential lifecycles

Acceptance Test-Driven Development

Acceptance Test-Driven Development (ATDD) defines acceptance criteria and tests during the creation of user stories. It is a collaborative approach that uses the whole team and the other relevant business stakeholders to contribute to the definition of acceptance criteria. User stories and example scenarios are used to consider how the software should behave. These decisions are documented as a set of acceptance tests before the coding begins.

ATDD involves the business stakeholders to ensure that the business acceptance criteria form the basis of development rather than the TDD which only focuses on functional criteria.

ATDD creates reusable tests which serve three purposes. These business-facing tests can be used by the developers to create code which meets the acceptance criteria of these tests. Secondly, they can be used by testing team for regression testing and are often automated using specific tools and are part of the continuous integration process. The third purpose is to use these tests for validation of feature behavior by the customer representatives. The results of these tests determine if the acceptance criteria are met for the feature.

Key exam take-out
• Acceptance criteria and tests are defined during the creation of user stories • Results of ATDD test cases quickly determines if the acceptance criteria are met • Helps developer collaborate with other stakeholders, including testers, to understand the functionality and define accurate unit tests focused on business needs • ATDD produces reusable tests for regression testing and confirms the software products desired behavior.

Behavior-Driven Development

Behavior-driven development allows developers to focus on testing the code based on the expected behavior of the software. As the tests are based on the exhibited behavior of the software, the tests are generally easier for other team members and stakeholders to understand.

BDD is usually done in very English- like language, which helps the domain experts and for non-technical stakeholders to understand.

As with all test-first approaches, BDD begins with the user story to identify examples (or scenarios) to which the software must respond to or cope with.

Specific behavior-driven development frameworks can be used to define

acceptance criteria based on the Given/When/Then format:

> **Given** some initial context,
>
> **When** an event occurs,
>
> **Then** ensure some outcomes.

As the statement structure and syntax are formally documented, software tools can generate the test cases for the developers. Behavior-driven development helps the developer collaborate with other stakeholders, including testers, to define accurate unit tests focused on business needs.

Example of a story that is described using the BDD method:

Story: Discounts on online shopping cart price for loyalty card customers

In order to increase the reward for loyal customers

I want to add 5-10% discounts on the final shopping cart price

Scenario 1: 5% discount for loyalty card customer

Given a loyalty card customer in online checkout page

When the shopping cart total is less than $100

Then 5% discount should be applied to the final shopping cart price

Scenario 2: 10% discount for loyalty card customer

Given a loyalty card customer in the online checkout page

When the shopping cart total is more than or equal to $100

Then 10% discount should be applied to the final shopping cart price

Key exam take-out

- In the BDD process the product owner or customer representatives specify the behavior they want to see in the system. The same is used to write the tests using frameworks that support BDD.
- Behavior-driven development frameworks define acceptance criteria based on the Given/When/Then format.
- As the tests are based on the exhibited behavior of the software, the tests are generally easier to understand for other team members and stakeholders

3.1.2 The Test Pyramid

The Test Pyramid is often used to illustrate different levels at which software may be tested. The levels of the pyramid from base to the top are:

- Unit
- Integration
- System
- Acceptance

The test pyramid emphasizes having a large number of tests at the lower levels (bottom of the pyramid) and, as development moves to the upper levels, the number of tests decreases (top of the pyramid).

Usually, unit and integration level tests are automated and are created using API-based tools. At the system and acceptance levels, automated tests are created using GUI-based tools. Testers can share the concept of test pyramid with other stakeholders to emphasize more automation for test on the lower levels.

The test pyramid is applicable only for **dynamic** (not static) testing. The concept is based on the principle of early testing (early the defect is found and eliminated in the project lifecycle the less is the cost of remediation).

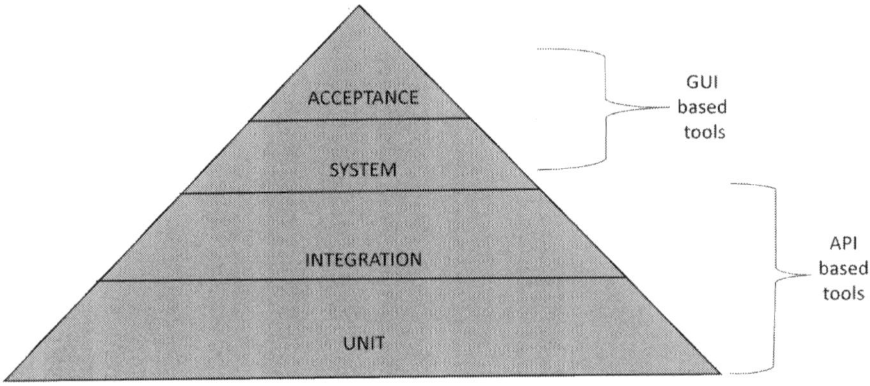

The Test Pyramid

Key exam take-out
• The pyramid represents larger number of tests at the lower levels (bottom of the pyramid) and a smaller number of tests when development moves to the upper levels (top of the pyramid) • Lower levels tests are often automated using API based tools • Higher levels tests are often automated using GUI based tools • It is based on the principle of early testing and applicable only for dynamic testing • Test pyramid can be helpful in planning the automation strategy for Agile teams

3.1.3 Testing Quadrants, Test Levels, and Testing Types

Brian Marick defined the Agile Testing Quadrants to bring clarity to the link between test levels and appropriate test types. Each of the four quadrants reflects the reason we do testing.

The **X-axis** shows the tests that **support the team** and **critique the product**, on the other hand, **Y-axis** shows the tests that are **business-facing** and **technology-facing**. Quadrant numbers are for identification only and the order in which they are numbered does not imply the sequence of testing.

The testing quadrants model and its variants help to ensure that all-important test types and test levels are included in the development lifecycle. This model also provides a way to differentiate and describe the types of tests to all stakeholders, including developers, testers, and business representatives.

In the testing quadrants, tests can be business (user) or technology (developer) facing. Some tests support the work done by the Agile team and confirm software behavior while other tests are used to verify the product. Tests can be fully manual, fully automated, a combination of manual and automated, or manual but supported by tools.

The four quadrants are as follows:

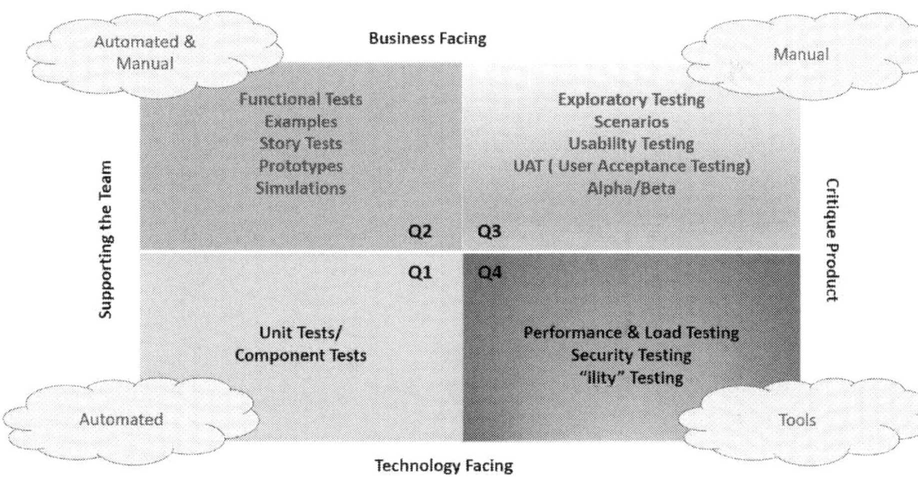

<u>**Agile Testing Quadrants**</u>

- **Quadrant Q1** is **unit level**, technology facing, and supports the developers. It contains **unit and component tests**. Unit tests are used to analyze and define software behavior and are written before the code is produced. Q1 tests should be automated and included in the continuous integration process.
- **Quadrant Q2** is **system-level**, business-facing, and confirms product behavior. This quadrant contains **functional tests, examples, story tests, user experience prototypes, and simulations**. These tests check the acceptance criteria and can be manual or automated. They are often created during the user story development and thus improve the quality of the stories. They are useful when creating automated regression test suites. Q2 includes both manual and/or automated test types.

- **Quadrant Q3** is **system or user acceptance level**, business-facing and contains tests that critique the product, using realistic scenarios and data. This quadrant contains **exploratory testing, scenarios, process flows, usability testing, user acceptance testing, alpha testing, and beta testing**. These tests are often manual and are user-oriented.
- **Quadrant Q4** is **technology facing** and contains tests that critique the product. It is the system or operational acceptance level and contains **performance, load, stress, and scalability tests, security tests, maintainability, memory management, compatibility and interoperability, data migration, infrastructure, and recovery testing**. These tests are often automated.

During any given iteration, tests from any or all quadrants may be required. The testing quadrants apply to **dynamic testing** rather than static testing.

Key exam take-out
• Testing quadrants align the test levels with the appropriate test types • Use of this model ensures that all-important test types and test levels are included in the development lifecycle • Helps to describe and differentiate types of tests to all stakeholders including developers, testers and business representatives • During any given iteration, tests from one, several or all quadrants may be required • The testing quadrants are only applicable to dynamic testing

3.1.4 The Role of a Tester

This subsection uses Scrum to illustrate the role of a tester in an Agile development environment.

Teamwork

Teamwork is the fundamental principle of Agile development. Agile emphasizes the whole-team approach consisting of developers, testers, and business representatives working together. Irrespective of the composition members are collectively responsible for the quality and delivery of the product.

From the tester's perspective, successful Scrum projects will require teams to be:

- **Cross-functional**: Each team member brings a different set of skills to the team. The team works together on test strategy, test planning, test specification, test execution, test evaluation, and test results reporting.
- **Empowered**: Self-organizing and self-managing, the team makes design and testing decisions in collaboration with the product owner and other teams if needed.
- **Co-located**: Testers sits together with the developers and the product owner.
- **Collaborative**: Testers work in partnership with other team members including stakeholders, product owner, scrum master and other teams to achieve the best outcomes.
- **Committed**: The tester is committed to question and evaluate the product's behavior and characteristics with respect to the expectations and needs of the customers and users.
- **Transparent**: Development and testing progress are made clearly visible on the Agile task board.
- **Credible**: The tester ensures the credibility of the strategy for testing, its implementation, and execution, otherwise, the stakeholders will not trust the test results. This is often done by providing information to the stakeholders about the testing process.
- **Open to feedback**: Feedback is an important aspect of being successful in any project, especially in Agile projects. Testers welcome constructive ideas and criticism. Retrospectives allow teams to learn from successes and failures.
- **Resilient**: Testing respond quickly to changes, like all other activities in Agile projects.

These practices maximize the likelihood of successful testing in Scrum projects.

Sprint Zero

Sprint zero is the first iteration of the project mainly reserved for preparation activities. This iteration is used for periods of planning and preparation for the release sprints that will deliver increments of the product. The length of this sprint is usually more than the normal sprint size. The tester collaborates with the team on the following activities in sprint zero:

- Identify the scope of the project (i.e. prepare the product backlog)
- Create an initial system architecture and high-level prototypes
- Specify the definition of "DONE"
- Create the task board (Agile board)
- Procure and install required tools for test management, defect management, test automation, and continuous integration.
- Create an initial test strategy for all test levels, addressing (among other topics) test scope, technical risks, test types, and coverage goals
- Undertake quality risk analysis
- Define test metrics to measure the test process, the progress of testing in the project and product quality
- Define when to continue or stop testing before delivering the system to the customer

Sprint zero sets the direction for what testing needs to achieve and how testing needs to achieve it throughout the sprints.

Integration

In Agile projects, the objective is to:

- Continuously deliver customer value:
    - In each sprint
    - At the end of the project.
- Continuous testing requires identifying all dependencies between functions and features
    - Integration strategy is helpful for this process
    - Important to identify all dependencies between underlying functions and features.

Test Planning

Since testing activities are fully integrated into the Agile project, test planning should start during the release planning session and be updated during each sprint. Planning should include the following tasks:

- Agreeing on the test scope, extent of testing, test and sprint goals
- Explain what's in and out of scope for testing
- Details of the test environment and what changes, data, tools, and configurations are needed for it
- Start date and frequency for test tasks
- Testing methods, techniques, tools, and data
- Dependencies
- Project and quality risks
- Priority-based on customer importance, risks, and dependencies
- Populating task board with tasks which have a length of 1-2 days of work

Agile Testing Practices

In addition to the activities described in Foundation Level syllabus many practices may be useful for testers in a scrum team, some of which include:

Pairing

It is a technique in which **two team members sit together at one workstation** to perform testing or other tasks within a sprint. Knowledge transfer and real-time reviewing are some of the benefits of this method. Examples include tester pairs with other testers to test a complex functionality, tester pair with developer to review the automation scripts, a developer pair with the product owner to understand the behavior of a particular functionality which can enable them to write behavior-driven tests.

Incremental test design

Test cases and test charters are gradually built from user stories and other test bases, starting from simple tests and moving towards more complex ones. Test charters are explained in detail in section 3.3.4.

Mind mapping

It is a useful tool for testers for recording discussions and to identify the test sessions. Mind maps can also be used to describe and illustrate concepts, such as test strategies and to describe test data.

Below is the example of using mind maps for brainstorming ideas to test a mail application.

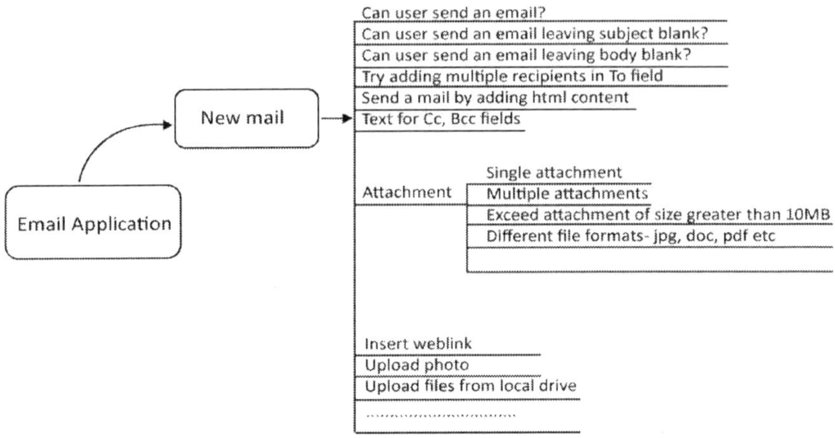

Mind map example

Exercise:

Consider the following Agile teams:

1. **Team A**: The team has agreed upon a Test process during the Release planning session, but the testers are not following it for some of the testing activities during the sprints.
2. **Team B**: The testers actively participate in all daily stand-up and planning meetings, but they are not invited to participate in the retrospective meetings happening at the end of each iteration.
3. **Team C**: The testers are reporting the testing progress to their Test Manager, but the team is not using an Agile task board for monitoring the development and testing tasks.
4. **Team D**: The testers are new to the Agile methodology and they are not able to keep up with the changes during each iteration.

Match the teams with the following organizational and behavioral practices they are lacking?

i. Transparent

ii. Open to Feedback

iii. Resilience

iv. Credible

Answer:

A. 1-iii, 2-ii, 3-i, 4-iv

B. 1-iii, 2-ii, 3-i, 4-iv

C. 1-iv, 2-i, 3-ii, 4-iii

D. 1-iv, 2-ii, 3-i, 4-iii

Option d) is correct see justification below

1. Testers in Team A are missing credibility.
2. Team B is not open to feedback as the testers are not participating in the retrospective meeting.
3. Team C is not as transparent as the progress of activities is not shared with the team.
4. Team D is not resilient as testers are not able to respond to changes.

3.2 Assessing Quality Risks and Estimating Test Effort

A typical objective of testing is to reduce the product risk to an acceptable level prior to release, this is applicable for traditional as well as Agile projects. Testers in Agile projects can use the same types of techniques used in traditional projects to identify quality or product risks, assess the associated level of risk, estimate the effort required to reduce those risks to an acceptable level, and then mitigate those risks through test design, implementation, and execution. As in Agile projects, the rate of changes is high and there are short iterations some adaptations of those techniques are required.

3.2.1 Assessing Quality Risks in Agile Projects

A risk can be defined as the possibility of an event in the future which has negative consequences. Risk is measured in terms of the likelihood of the event happening, and its potential impact.

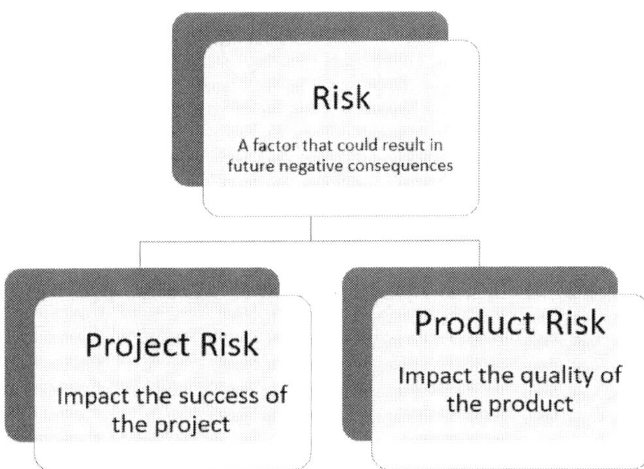

Product & Project risks

Project risks are risks that can affect the project success. **Product risks** are risks that a work product (e.g., a specification, component, system, or test) may fail to satisfy the legitimate needs of its users and/or stakeholders. Product risks are also called quality risks when they are associated with specific quality characteristics of a product (e.g., functional suitability, reliability, performance efficiency, usability, security, compatibility, maintainability, and portability). If the effect is on product quality, potential problems are referred to as quality risks or product risks.

In an Agile project, as in traditional projects, there are always contextual constraints that means that compromise is unavoidable. One of the many challenges in testing is the proper selection, allocation, and prioritization of test conditions. This includes determining the appropriate amount of effort to allocate in order to cover each condition with tests and sequencing the resulting tests in a way that optimizes the effectiveness and efficiency of the testing work to be done.

Testers commonly use risk identification, analysis, and risk mitigation strategies to make judgment on

- The extent of testing to be carried out
- Prioritization of testing
- Test techniques to be employed
- Selecting appropriate number of test cases for execution

In Agile projects, **quality risk analysis** takes place at two places.

- **During Release planning**: The business representative(s) may provide an overview of the features that will be included in the release and any perceived risks associated with them. The development team including testers will contribute to the discussions and help to identify and validate the risk and assess further ones.

- **During Iteration planning**: It is performed at a more detailed level. Once the tasks required to produce requirements are agreed then the tasks are placed on the task boards. Features associated with the tasks are then assessed for risk and those with greater risk may be started first as they will require more testing.

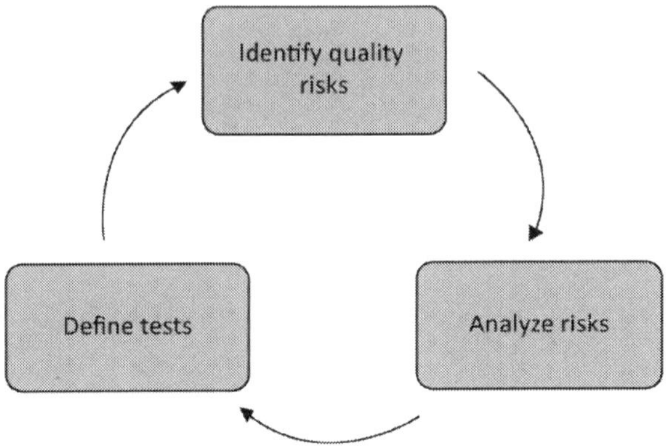

Quality Risk Analysis

An example of how the quality risk analysis process performed in the Agile project may be carried out during iteration planning is outlined in the following steps:

1. **Identify quality risk**
    a. The whole Agile team meets to identify the risks
    b. All current iteration backlog items are displayed
    c. The team discusses each item's quality characteristics and agrees on any quality risk that may emerge
2. **Analyze each risk**
    a. The team categorizes the risk. Example categories include product, project, business, and technical risks.
    b. The team assesses the likelihood that the risk will materialize and it's level of impact if it does.
3. **Define tests**
    a. The team determines the extent of testing required given the level of risk.
    b. The team selects appropriate test techniques to mitigate the risk based on the level of risk and the relevant quality characteristics (functionality, reliability, usability, etc).

In Agile projects, as changes are frequent, they may impact the plans. This includes the quality risk analysis which should be revisited periodically. Adjustments may be required where new risks have emerged, the level of existing risks change, and the effectiveness of existing risk mitigation activities may require examination and/or remediation.

All iterations start with iteration planning, which conclude with all the estimated tasks on a task board. These tasks can be prioritized based on the level of quality risk associated with them. Tasks associated with **higher risks should start earlier** and involve more rigorous testing and therefore more effort. Tasks associated with **lower risks should start later** and may involve less testing effort.

Some quality risks can be addressed even before testing begins. User stories with inadequate acceptance criteria, for example, can be viewed and properly elaborated to mitigate the risk that they pose.

The tester then designs, implements, and executes tests to mitigate the risks. This includes the totality of features, behaviors, quality characteristics, and attributes that affect customer, user, and stakeholder satisfaction.

Examples of quality risks for a system may include:

- Incorrect calculations in reports (a functional risk related to accuracy)
- Slow response to user input (a non-functional risk related to efficiency and response time)
- Difficulty in understanding screens and fields (a non-functional risk related to usability and understandability)
- Is the system able to operate satisfactorily with other systems (a risk related to compatibility)
- Is the system able to recover from hardware or software failures (a risk related to recoverability)

Exercise:

One of the Agile team is doing the quality risk analysis for the following user stories during the iteration planning session.

User Story 1: A program to calculate the salary for staff

User Story 2: A program to store customer credit card details.

User Story 3: A program to work on different operating systems.

Match the stories with their respective quality risk based on the information below:

Answer:

a) User Story 1: Security, User Story 2: Functional, User Story 3: Recoverability

b) User Story 1: Security, User Story 2: Performance, User Story 3: Compatibility

c) User Story 1: Functional, User Story 2: Security, User Story 3: Compatibility

d) User Story 1: Functional, User Story 2: Performance, User Story 3: Recoverability

Option c) is **correct** - see justification below

User Story 1: Incorrect salary calculation(accuracy) can result in functional risks

User Story 2: Storing customer sensitive information can result in security risks

User Story 3: Working on the different operating system can result in compatibility risks

Key exam take-out

- In Agile projects product risks are analyzed during both release and iteration planning
- Typical risk process involves identifying and analyzing the risks and then defines tests to mitigate it
- Risks are analyzed for functional as well as non-functional attributes
- Tasks associated with high risks should start earlier and may require more testing effort

3.2.2 Estimating Testing Effort Based on Content and Risk

During release planning, the Agile team estimates the effort required to complete the release, this also includes the testing effort.

The most common estimation techniques used in Agile projects is **planning poker** which is a consensus-based technique based on relative estimating. The values used for estimation can be Fibonacci sequence or any other progression of choice (e.g., shirt sizes ranging from extra-small to extra-large). The values represent the number of story points, effort days, or other units in which the team estimates.

The Fibonacci sequence (i.e. 0, 1, 2, 3, 5, 8, 13, 21, 34, 55, 89, ...) is recommended for the deck cards because the numbers in the sequence reflect that uncertainty grows proportionally with the size of the story. A high estimate usually means that the story is not well understood or should be broken down into multiple smaller stories.

Following are the sequence of activities for a planning poker session:

1. Customer or product owner explains the purpose of the user story and the business value it presents
2. The team discusses the user story for any clarifications
3. Each team member privately selects one card from the deck of cards to represent their estimate story points (generally a reference story is used, and the team member compares the story with the reference to arrive on a story point.)
4. The cards are revealed, and values are being compared
5. If all the estimates are of the same value, it is considered as final
6. For unequal estimation values, a discussion is started; usually, the team member with the highest and the lowest value will provide their reasoning
7. Then another round is 'played' until an agreement is reached either by consensus or by applying rules (e.g. use the median, average or use the highest score) to limit the number of poker rounds

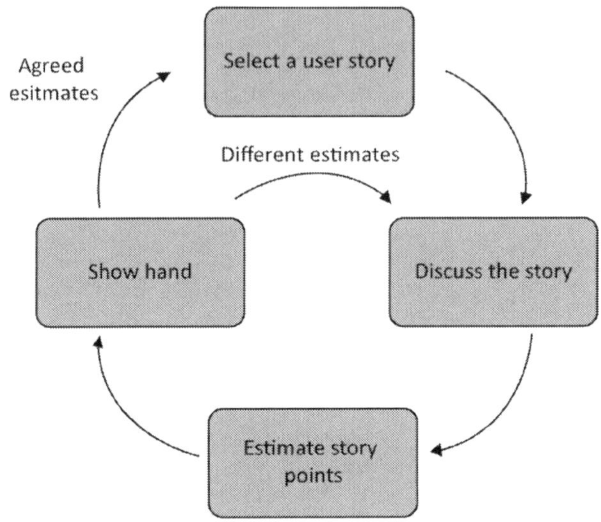

Planning Poker

Benefits of the whole team estimation method:

- Discussion of the story during poker planning helps the team gets the common understanding of the features
- A higher estimate means the story is too complex and should be split up into smaller stories if possible

Exercise:

Consider the following user story:

"As an online Shopper, I want to delete items from my shopping cart so that I don't purchase items that I decide I don't want before the final checkout"

The Agile team is doing the estimation for this story. The tester has asked the following questions to the product owner to get a better understanding of the functionality for estimation purposes.

Which of the tester's questions is NOT relevant for the estimation process?

Answer:

a) Tester: "What business benefit does this story deliver?"
b) Tester: "What is the worst thing that could happen with this feature?"
c) Tester: "How will the end-user actually use this feature?"
d) Tester: "What is the business priority for this user story?"

Option d) is correct – This is not relevant. The business priority of the user story will not help in estimating the user story.

Key exam take-out

- Planning poker is a consensus-based technique for estimation
- The team assesses the story point based on the relative size of each task associated with the story
- Aspects such as development and testing effort, the complexity of the story, risk level and the scope of testing play a key role in the estimation.
- Assessment/evaluation of the effort can be done using story points by means of planning poker cards using Fibonacci numbers or T-shirt sizes: (**S**)mall, (**M**)edium, (**L**)arge and (**XL**) extra large

3.3 Techniques in Agile Projects

Many of the test techniques and testing levels that apply to traditional projects can also be applied to Agile projects. However, for Agile projects, there are some specific considerations and variances in test techniques, terminologies, and documentation that should be considered.

3.3.1 Acceptance Criteria, Adequate Coverage, and Other Information for Testing

Agile projects document requirements as user stories in a prioritized backlog at the start of the project. These stories are typically short, functional and usually follow a standard format such as the one presented in Section 1.2.2. Non-functional requirements, such as usability and performance, are also important and can be specified as unique user stories or part of other functional user stories. Non-functional requirements may follow a predefined format or standard, such as [ISO25000] or an industry-specific standard.

Test Bases

User stories are an important test basis. Other possible test bases include:

- Code
- The architecture of the system
- Detailed design
- Existing functions, features, and quality characteristics of the system
- Experience from previous projects
- Information on defects from existing and previous projects
- User profiles or personas (context, system configurations, and user-behavior)
- A categorization of defects in a defect taxonomy
- Any relevant standards such as MISRAC for safety-critical automotive systems
- Quality risks

During each iteration, developers create code which implements the functions and features described in the user stories. The code for the user stories is verified and validated via acceptance testing. To be testable, acceptance criteria should address the following topics where relevant:

- **Functional behavior**: What the system does, which will be externally observables (e.g. customers can download a report).

- **Quality characteristics**: How the system performs the specified behavior. The characteristics may also be referred to as quality attributes or non-functional requirements. Common quality characteristics are performance, reliability, usability, etc. (e.g. response time below 2 seconds).
- **Scenarios/use cases**: A sequence of actions between an external actor (often a user) and the system in order to accomplish a specific goal or business task. (e.g. customer (actor) perform login and logout functions)
- **Business rules:** Activities that can only be performed in the system under certain conditions defined by outside procedures and constraints. (e.g. customer credit checks for personal loans more than $5,000)
- **External interfaces**: Descriptions of the connections between the system to be developed and the outside world. External interfaces, interface to other systems, etc.
- **Constraints**: Any project, design or implementation requirements that limit or confine development within prescribed boundaries (e.g. the system must be implemented by certain time to meet the regulatory requirements).
- **Data definitions**: The customer may describe the format, data type, allowed values, and default values for a data item in the composition of a complex business data structure (e.g. dates in DD-MM-YYYY format).

Other information which can be relevant for the tester may include:

- How the system is supposed to work and be used
- The system interfaces that can be accessed to test the system
- Are the testing tools adequate for testing needs
- Does the tester have enough knowledge and skill to perform the necessary tests

Testers will often find that they need additional information (e.g. code coverage) throughout the project and should work collaboratively with the rest of the team members to obtain that information. Relevant information plays a part in determining whether a particular activity can be considered done. This concept of the definition of done is critical in Agile projects and applies in a number of different ways as discussed in the following sub-subsections.

Definition of Done -Test Levels

Each test level has its own definition of done. The following list provides examples that may be relevant for the different test levels.

Unit testing

- Target 100% decision coverage- any infeasible paths must be subject to the detailed review
- Static analysis performed on all code
- No outstanding major defects (based on agreed definitions)
- No known unacceptable technical debt remaining in the design and the code
- All code, unit tests, and unit test results reviewed
- All unit tests automated
- Important characteristics are within agreed limits (e.g., performance)

Integration testing

- All functional requirements tested, including both positive and negative tests, with the number of tests based on size, complexity, and risks
- All interfaces between units tested
- All quality risks covered according to the agreed extent of testing
- No unresolved major defects (prioritized according to risk and importance)
- All defects found are reported
- All regression tests automated, where possible, with all automated tests stored in a common repository

System testing

- End-to-end tests of user stories, features, and functions
- All user personas covered
- The most important quality characteristics of the system covered (e.g., performance, robustness, reliability)
- Testing is done in a production-like environment(s), including all hardware and software for all supported configurations, to the extent possible
- All quality risks covered according to the agreed extent of testing
- All regression tests automated, where possible, with all automated tests stored in a common repository
- All defects found are reported and possibly fixed
- No unresolved major defects (prioritized according to risk and importance)

Definition of Done-User Stories

The definition of done for user stories may be determined by the following criteria:

- The user stories selected for the iteration are complete, understood by the team, and have detailed, testable acceptance criteria
- All the elements of the user story are specified and reviewed, including the user story acceptance tests, have been completed
- Tasks necessary to implement and test the selected user stories have been identified and estimated by the team

Definition of Done-Features

The definition of done for features, which may span multiple user stories or epics may include:

- All constituent user stories, with acceptance criteria, are defined and approved by the customer
- The design is complete, with no known technical debt
- The code is complete, with no known technical debt or unfinished refactoring
- Unit tests have been performed and have achieved the defined level of coverage
- Integration tests and system tests for the feature have been performed according to the defined coverage criteria
- No major defects remain to be corrected
- Feature documentation is complete, which may include release notes, user manuals, and online help functions

Definition of Done-Iterations

The definition of done for the iteration may include the following:

- All features for the iteration are ready and individually tested according to the feature level criteria
- Any non-critical defects that cannot be fixed within the constraints of the iteration added to the product backlog and prioritized
- Integration of all features for the iteration completed and tested
- Documentation written, reviewed, and approved at this point; the software is potentially shippable.

Definition of Done-Releases

The definition of done for a release, which may span multiple iterations, may include the following areas:

- **Coverage**: All relevant test basis elements for all contents of the release have been covered by testing. The adequacy of the coverage is determined by what is new or changed, its complexity and size, and the associated risks of failure.
- **Quality**: The number of defects found per day or per transaction is called the defect intensity and the number of defects found compared to the number of user stories is called defect density. Both of these parameters should remain within acceptable limits. The consequences of these limits, which may raise the residual level of risk, shall be fully understood and accepted.
- **Time**: If the pre-determined delivery date has been reached, the business considerations associated with releasing and not releasing need to be considered.
- **Cost**: The estimated lifecycle cost should be used to calculate the return on investment for the delivered system (i.e. the calculated development and maintenance cost should be considerably lower than the expected total sales of the product). The main part of the lifecycle cost often comes from maintenance after the product has been released, this may be due to the defects which were not caught during testing and escaped to production.

Exercise:

One of the Agile team is building a new system to replace a legacy system. The new system will use a totally new technology as the old technology of the legacy system is no longer supported by vendors. For the testing of this new system, which of the following would best provide relevant information to support testing activities in addition to the user stories?

i. Experience in testing the legacy system.
ii. Performance metrics from the legacy system.
iii. Architecture diagrams for the legacy system.
iv. Customer profiles from the legacy system.
v. Defects from the existing legacy system.

Answer:

a) i, iii, iv, v
b) i, ii, iii, v
c) i, iv, v
d) All of the above

Option a) is correct – see below

i. This is helpful to understand the application and to write E2E test cases.
ii. This is not helpful because as a new relational database is being introduced, baselines should be obtained with similar technology or defined performance requirements for this type of technology.
iii. This is helpful to understand the application and to write test cases.
iv. This is helpful to write test cases.
v. This is helpful during the risk analysis phase.

3.3.2 Applying Acceptance Test-Driven Development

As discussed, earlier Acceptance test-driven development (ATDD) is a test-first approach where test cases are created prior to implementing the user story. The test cases are created by the Agile team, including the developer, the tester, and the business representatives. They can be manual or automated.

ATDD uses a business-focused approach. This approach has four steps and is explained below.

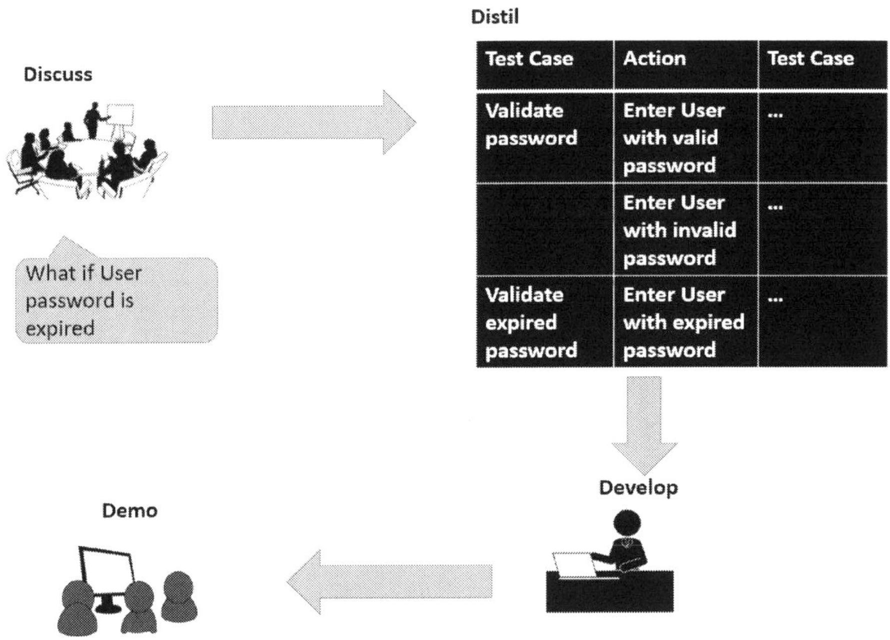

Acceptance Test-Driven Development cycle

1. Discuss

The first step is a **specification workshop** where the user story is analyzed, discussed, and possibly re-written based on the discussion between developers, testers, and business representatives. Any incompleteness, ambiguities or errors in the user story are fixed during this process.

2. Distil

The next step is to **create the tests**. This can be done by the team together or by the tester individually. They convert the set of acceptance tests for the user story. These tests are examples that describe the specific characteristics of the user story. They are created from the perspective of the user and the observable behavior of the software. These examples help the team to implement the user story correctly.

Positive tests

Usually, the first set of tests describe the standard behavior without exception or error conditions. They include the order of activities that are to be executed if everything goes as expected.

Negative tests

After the positive path tests are done, the team focus on negative path tests. The team should also cover exceptions, error handling and non-functional quality characteristics (e.g. performance, usability).

Example:

An application requires a valid age entry between 18 and 65 years (both inclusive)

- Positive tests: Entry of 18, 30 or 65 as age
- Negative tests: Entry of 17, -5 or ABC as age

Tests are expressed in a way that every stakeholder is able to understand, containing sentences in natural language involving the necessary preconditions, inputs, and the related outputs.

The examples must cover all the characteristics of the user story and should not add any new characteristics to the story. This means that an example should not exist which describes an aspect of the user story not documented in the story itself. In addition, no two examples should describe the same characteristics of the user story.

3. Develop

The **developers now code**, in the manner of TDD, to meet the examples (pass the tests) produced in the Distil step.

4. Demo

Finally, **the team showcases the function/feature** to the relevant business stakeholders who will provide feedback which may prompt more discussions (Step 1)

Explaining Testable Acceptance Criteria to Business Stakeholders

Business stakeholders may require help to understand the need for and the definition of testable acceptance criteria.

It's helpful to:

- Use examples of testable acceptance criteria and untestable acceptance criteria so that the difference between verifiable criteria and unverifiable criteria are illustrated through the example
- Use examples of testable acceptance criteria and untestable acceptance criteria that are relevant to their business domain and requirements
- Highlight the specificity and measurability of the testable criteria and compare it to the subjectivity of the untestable criteria
- Use terminology which the business stakeholders can understand
- Ensure that the business stakeholders understand that the goal is to achieve a definition with metrics and when tested can be assessed in terms of:
  - Yes, the system behaved in that way

  OR

  - No, the system did not behave in that way-which would mean a defect.

Examples:

Testable acceptance criteria	Untestable acceptance criteria
The data entry screen should have a tabbing sequence to navigate from top to bottom and left to right	The system should be user-friendly
The system main page should open in less than 2 seconds	The system should respond quickly
The system should recover from backup within 30 seconds time after failures	The system should recover from backup within a reasonable time after failures
The system should be available 24 hours Monday to Friday	The system should be available all the time
The new changes should be available to the users within 10 minutes of new deployment	The new changes are available to the users as soon as possible

Exercise:

Consider the following User Story regarding the search functionality of the health insurance website:

"As a customer, I can find a health care provider based on the Region, Category, or suburb information"

Which of the following can be considered as relevant acceptance test cases?

i. The search window should display with a reasonable time.
ii. Select the Region from the dropdown and click the Search button
iii. Select the Category from the dropdown and click the Search button
iv. Select the suburb from the dropdown and click the Search button
v. Select the Region, category, and suburb from the dropdown and click the search button
vi. Select the health care provider type and click the search button.

Answer:

i, ii, iv

ii, iii, iv

ii, iv, vi

iii, iv, vi

Option b) is c**orrect** – see justification below.

i. Incorrect – The user story does not mention performance requirements.
ii. **Correct** – This test is specific to the search service provider function.
iii. **Correct** – This test is specific to the search service provider function.
iv. **Correct**- This test is specific to the search service provider function.
v. Incorrect – The user story is specific to search based on either Region, Category, or suburb information. The question is specific to Either/OR not Any/All
vi. Incorrect- The user story is specific to the search based on the Region, Category, or suburb information.

Key exam take-out
• The ATDD starts with base examples and open questions which become the foundation of tests • These examples help the team to correctly implement the user story • The tests are examples, that describe the specific characteristics of the user story • The test cases created should be reviewed by business representatives

3.3.3 Functional and Non-Functional Black Box Test Design

Black-box test design techniques (also called behavioral or behavior-based techniques) are used to derive and select test conditions or test cases, based on the analysis of the test basis documentation.

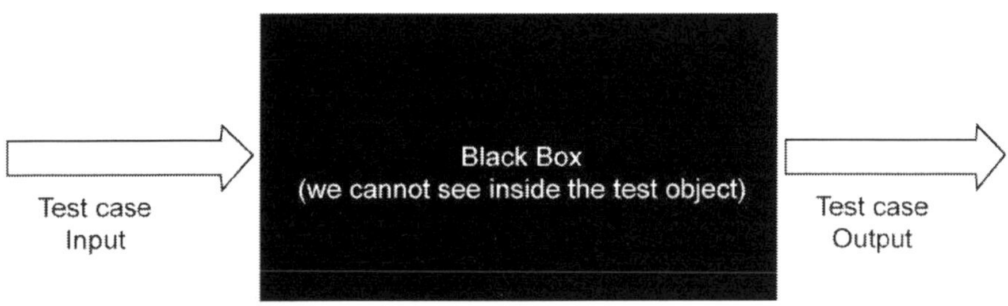

Black-box testing

These techniques concentrate on the inputs and outputs of the test object without reference to its internal structure. They can be used for both functional and non-functional testing.

Common features of black-box test techniques:

- Test conditions, test cases, and test data are derived from a test basis that may include software requirements, specifications, use cases, and user stories
- Test cases may be used to detect gaps between the requirements and the implementation of the requirements, as well as deviations from the requirements
- Coverage is measured based on the items tested in the test basis and the technique applied to the test basis

In Agile testing, many tests are created by testers concurrently with the developer's programming activities. Just as the developers are programming based on the user stories and acceptance criteria, so are the testers creating tests based on user stories and their acceptance criteria. Though some experience-based tests, such as exploratory tests are created later during test execution. Traditional black box test design techniques from the ISTQB Foundation Level syllabus such as equivalence partitioning, boundary value analysis, decision tables, and state transition testing are all relevant in the Agile context and can be used to test both functional and non-functional requirements. For example:

Functional: State transition test design to create tests that ensure an amount is not deducted from customer account if the order is cancelled

Non- functional: Boundary value analysis to test auto logout functionality after a period of inactivity performance or reliability requirements

As the acceptance criteria are developed in the iteration shortly before the user story is implemented. Therefore, when developers are coding for the story, in parallel the testers will often create tests for the same story (based on the same artifacts).

Exercise:

Given the following user story:

"An application for the parcel post service calculates the postage rate for parcels up to 10 kg based on the following criteria:

- Standard postage rate for weight under 1 kg
- The postage rate is $20 for weight more than 1 kg and under 2 kg
- The postage rate is flat $35 for weight more than 5 kg

Which of the following is the best black box test design technique for the user story?

a) Boundary Value Analysis
b) Decision tables
c) State Transition testing
d) Use Case Testing

Option a) is correct – Boundary Value Analysis (BVA) will be the best option for this story as the testing involves verifying the postage rate at boundary values.

Key exam take-out

- Tester in Agile projects can use following black-box design techniques to design tests:
  - Equivalence partitioning (EP)
  - Boundary value analysis (BVA)
  - Decision tables
  - State-based tests
- Black-box test design techniques are also suitable for creating tests for non-functional quality characteristics
- Non-functional requirements should be documented as part of the user story

3.3.4 Exploratory Testing and Agile Testing

In exploratory testing, test cases are not pre-defined but design, execution, test logging, and learning are carried out dynamically during test execution.

In exploratory testing tester dynamically adjusts test goals during execution and prepares only lightweight documentation. The test results help in learning more about the system, and to create tests for the areas that may require more testing.

It is widely used in Agile projects due to the **limited time available for test analysis** and also due to the **limited details in the user stories**. In order to achieve the best results, as part of a reactive testing strategy, exploratory testing and experience-based techniques should be blended with other testing strategies such as analytical risk-based testing, analytical requirements-based testing, model-based testing, and regression-averse testing. Test strategies and test strategy blending are discussed in the Foundation Level syllabus.

In exploratory testing, test design and test execution occur at the same time, guided by a prepared test charter. **A test charter** provides the test conditions to cover during a time-boxed testing session. During exploratory testing, the results of the most recent tests guide the next test. The tester can use the white box and black box techniques to design the tests while performing testing.

A test charter may include the following information:

- **Actor**: The system user
- **Purpose**: Includes the objective that the actor wants to achieve (test conditions)
- **Setup**: What needs to be in place in order to start the test execution
- **Priority**: Relative importance of this charter, based on the priority of the associated user story or the risk level
- **Reference**: Specifications (e.g., user story), risks, or other information sources
- **Data**: Required to carry out the charter
- **Activities**: a list of possible scenarios that the actor may engage in and possible tests (positive and negative)
- **Oracle notes**: How to evaluate the product to determine correct results (e.g., to capture what happens on the screen and compare to what is written in the user's manual)
- **Variations**: Alternative actions and evaluations to complement the ideas described under activities

A tester must ask **relevant questions about what to test**. These will be contextually dependent but can include the following:

- What is most important to find out about the system?
- In what way may the system fail?
- What happens if.....?
- What should happen when.....?
- Are customer needs, requirements, and expectations fulfilled?
- Is the system possible to install (and remove if necessary) in all supported upgrade paths?

A **set of heuristics can be applied when testing**. A heuristic offers a set of guiding "rules of thumb" testing and to evaluating the results. Examples include:

- **CRUD**: Create, Read, Update, Delete
- **Follow the Data**: Actions that enter, search, report, export, import, etc.
- **Configuration variations**: Change configuration data
- **Constraints**: Violate them. Leave mandatory fields null, etc.
- **Interruptions**: Log off, shut down, or reboot, disconnect, etc.
- **Multi-user**: CRUD from multiple logins

Agile encourages lightweight documentation but it is important to record the test flow. Otherwise, it would be difficult to go back and see how a problem in the system was found. This may be captured in test/task management tools or on the task board so that interested parties have visibility of the testing progress. The following list provides examples of information that may be useful to document:

- **Test coverage**: Data used, how much has been covered, and how much is remaining
- **Evaluation notes**: Observations during testing, do the system and feature under test seem to be stable, were any defects found, what is planned as the next step according to the current observations, and any other list of ideas
- **Risk/strategy list**: Risks covered and remaining. Does the original strategy still seem appropriate or changes are required?
- **Issues, questions and anomalies**: Unexpected behavior, questions regarding the efficiency of the approach, concerns about the ideas/test attempts, test environment, test data, misunderstanding of the function, test script or the system under test
- **Actual behavior**: Recording of the actual behavior of the system that needs to be saved (e.g., video, screen captures, output data files)

To manage exploratory testing, a method called **session-based test management** can be used. A session is defined as an uninterrupted period of testing which could last from 60 to 120 minutes. Test sessions include the following:

- Survey session (to learn how it works)
- Analysis session (evaluation of the functionality or characteristics)
- Deep coverage (corner cases, scenarios, interactions)

Exercise:

In one of the Agile projects, testers have been asked to plan exploratory testing. Which of the following approach is NOT correct for Exploratory testing?

a) Testers should do the risk analysis and then test the critical things they think could go wrong or the potential problems that will make people unhappy.

b) Testers should test based on the model of how software should behave. The functions which the customers are more interested in should be tested first.

c) Testers should test based on their past experience of how similar systems failed in predictable patterns. These experiences can be refined into a test and explored.

d) Tests should not be planned as the testers have already tested these stories and should progress the test based on their intuition.

Option d) is NOT correct. There is a plan required for exploratory testing.

The rest of the options are correct for exploratory testing.

Key exam take-out
• In exploratory testing test design and test execution occurs at the same time • Exploratory testing is guided by test charter which provides the test conditions to cover during a time-boxed testing session • The tester must ask relevant questions about what to test before the start of exploratory tests to make effectively use of the testing session • For exploratory testing to be effective testing is done in defined session while last for 60-120 mins. (session-based test management)

3.4 Tools in Agile Projects

Test software tools used in traditional projects are relevant also to Agile based projects. Not all tools are used the same way and some tools have more relevance for Agile projects than they have in traditional projects. Some Agile teams opt for an all-inclusive tool (e.g., application lifecycle management or task management) that provides features relevant to Agile development. They support user story cards, task boards, burndown charts, and other collaborative tools. Configuration management tools are important to testers in Agile teams due to the high number of automated tests at all levels and the need to store and manage the associated automated test artifacts.

In addition to the tools described in the ISTQB Foundation Level syllabus, testers on Agile projects are likely to use tools for:

- Tasks management and tracking
- Communication and information sharing
- Configuration management
- Test design, implementation, and execution
- Cloud computing and virtualization

3.4.1 Task Management and Tracking Tools

Most of the Agile teams use physical story/task boards to manage and track user stories, tests, and other tasks throughout each sprint. To visualise the movement of the user stories and tasks some Agile teams may also use application lifecycle management and task management software, including electronic task boards. e.g. JIRA.

These tools serve the following purposes:

- Record the stories with relevant development and testing tasks
- Collect the individual team members estimations, calculation of the necessary **total effort** for the implementation of the story
- Combining the development tasks and test tasks with the same story, to provide a **complete picture** of the team's effort required to implement the story
- **Record the status** of the tasks after each update by the Agile team members
- Visual representation of the current state of each user story, the iteration, and the release through metrics, charts, and dashboards so all the stakeholders can quickly check the status

- Integration with configuration management tools for automatic recording of code check-ins and builds against tasks **automated status updates** for tasks

3.4.2 Communication and Information Sharing Tools

As one of the Agile principles' states that most efficient and effective way of conveying information is by **face-to-face conversation**. It should be the first choice of communication medium in Agile development projects. However, if the teams are geographically distributed technology can be used as supplement ways for communication.

In addition to verbal communication, e-mail and documents, Agile teams often use three additional types of tools to support communication and information sharing:

- **Wiki** -an online knowledge base for different project aspects
- **Instant messaging**- for individual and group chats including conference and video chats
- **Desktop sharing**- for easy review and demos

1. **Wiki** allows teams to build and share an **online knowledge base** on various aspects of the project, including the following:
    - **Product feature diagrams, feature discussions, prototype diagrams**, photos of the whiteboard (storyboard) which can be used in team meetings and workshops
    - **Development/testing tools and techniques** which can be shared with other team members
    - **Metrics, charts, and dashboards** related to product status (if wiki is integrated with build and task management system the status is automatically updated)
    - **Conversations between team members** which can be helpful for other team members e.g. discussion regarding the feature between the developers and product owner

2. **Instant messaging**, audio teleconferencing, and video chat tools provide the following benefits:
    - **Direct real-time communication** between team members
    - Involve **distributed teams in team activities** e.g. stand-up, planning meetings.
    - Removing and **reducing cost constraints** that could impede the communication in distributed teams

3. **Desktop sharing and capturing tools** provide the following benefits:
    - **Product demonstrations, code reviews, and pairing** can occur for distributed teams
    - **Capturing product demonstrations** at the end of each iteration which can be integrated to team's wiki

These tools should be used to complement and extend and not replace face-to-face communication in Agile teams.

3.4.3 Software Build and Distribution Tools

Daily build and deployment of software is a key practice in Agile projects. This requires the use of continuous integration tools and builds distribution tools.

3.4.4 Configuration Management Tools

Configuration management software is used to store all project work product which includes

- **Business-oriented work products** - requirement specifications, user documentation
- **Development work products** - development documents, source code, automated unit tests
- **Test work product** - Test artifacts, manual and automated tests, and test results

Version management is done through **Version Control Systems** (VCS). There are two options:

- **Centralized** source control systems
- **Distributed** version control systems

For evaluating the suitability of a VCS for an individual Agile project, the following factors should be considered:

- The team size and structure
- Location of team members (e.g. co-located or distributed)
- Requirements to integrate with other tools used by the team

Advantage of using configuration management tools:

- It allows traceability (e.g. which versions of the software was tested with which versions of the tests)
- It allows for rapid change of work product without losing historical information.

3.4.5 Test Design, Implementation, and Execution Tools

Some tools are useful to Agile testers at specific points in the software testing process. While most of these tools are not new or specific to Agile, they provide important capabilities given the rapid change of Agile projects.

- **Test design tools**: These tools help the Agile testers to **design the test cases** and ensure the coverage.

  Mind maps tools are frequently used for design and defining tests for a new features in Agile projects.

- **Test case management tools:** The types of tools are used by the testers and other team members of the Agile team to **manage the test cases** for different phases. These tools may be part of the whole team's application lifecycle management or task management tool. Application Lifecycle Management (ALM) is a tool that can be used to manage the test case other than providing visibility into the current state of the application, especially with distributed teams.

- **Test data preparation and generation tools**: During dynamic testing test data is required to execute the test scripts. The tester needs to create this data, which is a time-consuming process, other options include using the production data and use data masking to sanitize and protect production data, so it is safe to use for testing.

  There are tools that can help the testers to **generate test data** and are very cost/time effective where the required volume of data is high or multiple combinations of data are needed. These tools can also help re-define the database structure due to requirement change and refactor the data generation scripts. Some test data preparation tools use production data as a source and use techniques for data masking so the data can be used for testing. Other test data preparation tools provide validation support for large data inputs or outputs.

- **Test data load tools**: After data has been generated for testing, it needs to be **loaded into the application**. Manual data entry is inefficient, time-consuming and error-prone, tools are more reliable and efficient. Many of the data generator tools include an integrated data load component otherwise the data can be bulk loaded using the database management systems.

- **Automated test execution tools**: There are test execution tools that support test first approaches, such as Behavior- Driven Development (BDD), Test-Driven Development (TDD), and Acceptance Test-Driven Development. These tools allow testers and business staff to express the expected system behavior natural language using keywords or tables.

  Jbehave is one of the tools which is used for Behavior-Driven Development (BDD).

- **Exploratory test tools**: Exploratory testing is done without any formal test cases, so it is difficult to replicate the steps if any defects are found. There are tools that **record the activity performed during exploratory test** sessions, as they record the actions taken. This is useful when a defect is found, as the actions are taken before the failure occurred have been captured and can be used to report the defect to the developers. These steps can also be added to the automated test suite.

3.4.6 Cloud Computing and Virtualization Tools

Virtualization allows a single physical resource (server) to operate as many separate, smaller resources. When virtual machines or cloud instances are used, teams can easily create multiple instances of development and test environment for development and testing.

Advantage of using virtualization tools:

- The delays for setting up physical servers can be reduced
- The new server can be quickly provisioned, and the existing servers can be restored using snapshot functionality.
- The tester can take the snapshot of the servers at the point when a defect is found, this can help the developers in debugging activities
- Virtualization reduced the cost associated with team waiting for resources, power consumption and physical space.

Cloud computing allows the usage of virtualized resources in external physical hardware which is hosted by a supplier.

Advantage of cloud computing:

- It allows the cost management for the team as the service is paid based on the demand model
- It avoids large capital expenditure on hardware and upgrades

- It provides flexibility for the infrastructure demand when the business requirements are changing
- It is easy to cope up with demand by scaling up without expanding their own infrastructure
- It allows the team to utilize tools available on cloud without need of specialized people for setup

Key exam take-out
• Tool usage is driven from the Agile principles; keep it simple and less documentation • **Tasks management & tracking tools**- real-time status of tasks carried by the Agile team members • **Communication and information sharing**- enable efficient & effective communication between team member • **Configuration management**- stores and manages work products • **Test design, implementation, and execution**- help the team in the testing tasks • **Cloud computing and virtualization**- enables the team to have multiple instances of environment for development and testing tasks

3.5 Relevant glossary terms and keywords

Glossary term	Definition
Acceptance criteria	The criteria that a component or system must satisfy in order to be accepted by a user, customer, or other authorized entity.
Exploratory testing	An approach to testing whereby the testers dynamically design and execute tests based on their knowledge, exploration of the test item and the results of previous tests.
Performance testing	Testing to determine the performance of a software product.
Product risk	A risk impacting the quality of a product.
Quality risk	A product risk related to a quality characteristic.
Regression testing	Testing of a previously tested component or system following modification to ensure that defects have not been introduced or have been uncovered in unchanged areas of the software, as a result of the changes made.
Test approach	The implementation of the test strategy for a specific project.
Test charter	Documentation of test activities in session-based exploratory testing.
Test estimation	The calculated approximation of a result related to various aspects of testing (e.g., effort spent, completion date, costs involved, number of test cases, etc.) which is usable even if input data may be incomplete, uncertain, or noisy
Test execution automation	The use of software, e.g., capture/playback tools, to control the execution of tests, the comparison of actual results to expected results, the setting up of test preconditions, and other test control and reporting functions.
Test strategy	Documentation that expresses the generic requirements for testing one or more projects run within an organization, providing detail on how testing is to be performed, and is aligned with the test policy.
Test-driven development	A way of developing software where the test cases are developed, and often automated, before the software is developed to run those test cases.
Unit test framework	A tool that provides an environment for unit or component testing in which a component can be tested in isolation or with suitable stubs and drivers. It also provides other support for the developer, such as debugging capabilities

3.6 Summary

TDD:

First create automated unit test cases then start coding.

ATDD:

Create acceptance criteria in collaboration with the whole team.

BTDD:

Define acceptance criteria based on the given/when/then format.

Test pyramid

More tests at lower test levels, fewer at the higher test level

Testing quadrants:

- Unit level, system level, user acceptance level, operational acceptance level
- **Q1** – Unit level, high degree of automation
- **Q2** – System level, can be manual or automated
- **Q3** – System acceptance or user acceptance level, mostly manual
- **Q4** – System acceptance or operational acceptance level, mostly automated/tools supported

Role of the tester in Agile projects

- **Teamwork** - Testers and other team members are equally responsible for the quality
- **Sprint zero** - planning and preparation iteration
- **Integration** -Continuously deliver customer value
- **Test planning** - Starts during the release planning session and updated during each Sprint
- **Agile test practices** - Pairing, incremental test design, mind mapping

Quality Risks assessment:

- Quality risk analysis is done at release and iteration planning
- Quality risk analysis process:
  - **Identify quality risks**- whole team brainstorm
  - **Analyze each risk**- categorizing the risks
  - **Define tests**- testing required to mitigate identified risks, the higher the risk the more testing effort and early testing

Planning poker:

- Frequently used Agile estimation method for story points
- Tester ask relevant questions during planning poker to properly estimate story

Relevant Information to support Testing activity

- Along with user stories testers may use other test bases for testing i.e. code, design diagrams, existing features, and functions, defect information, user profiles, etc

Definition of Done (DOD)

- Definition of Done (DOD) is used in Agile projects to determine if the particular activity can be considered complete
- DOD applies to test levels, user stories, features, iterations, and releases

Applying Acceptance Test-Driven Development (ATDD)

- ATDD is a business-focused approach and has discuss, distil, develop and demo steps

Testable Acceptance Criteria

- Acceptance criteria in the user story should be checked for testability

Functional and non-functional black box design

- Black box techniques can be used to design test for functional and non-functional tests

Exploratory Testing

- Exploratory testing is widely used in Agile projects due to limited time for testing and limited information in user stories
- Test charters are used to guide exploratory testing and test session are used for uninterrupted testing in defined timeframes.

Tools in Agile project

- **Tasks management & tracking tools**- real-time status of tasks carried by the Agile team members
- **Communication and information sharing-** enable efficient & effective communication between team member
- **Configuration management-** stores and manages work products
- **Test design, implementation, and execution-** help the team in the testing design, implementation and execution tasks
- **Cloud computing and virtualization-** enable the team to have multiple instances of environment for development and testing activities

3.7 Quiz

Question 1

Which of the following is false about Acceptance-Test-driven-Development (ATDD)?

Answer:

A. Acceptance criteria and tests are defined during the creation of user stories
B. The focus of the test written for ATDD is based on the developer's perspective
C. Developers and testers collaborate with other stakeholders to define acceptance criteria
D. Developers write the code to meet the defined acceptance criteria

Question 2

The concept of the Test Pyramid is related to which of the following?

Answer:

A. Remove defects as early as possible
B. All test levels are required for Agile software development
C. Static testing is more effective in finding defects
D. Regression risk increases with each new functionality implemented

Question 3

Which of the following statements are true with respect to testing quadrants?

1. Testing quadrants ensure that all-important test types and test levels are included in the development lifecycle
2. Testing quadrants can be used to check the test coverage metric
3. Testing quadrants align the test levels with appropriate test types
4. Testing quadrants are used for risk analysis during release and iteration planning

Answer:

A. 1 and 3

B. 2 and 3

C. 2 and 4

D. 1 and 4

Question 4

The testers focus on which of the following tasks during sprint zero in Agile projects?

i. Help the team in preparation of product backlog

ii. Create testing tasks for user stories

iii. Help the team in the quality risk analysis

iv. Create the initial test strategy for all test levels

Answer:

A. i, ii, iii

B. i, iii, iv

C. i, iii

D. All of the above

Question 5

Which of the following is NOT done during the risk assessment process?

Answer:

A. Categorize the risk

B. Assess the likelihood of risk

C. Check the impact of risk

D. Selecting the appropriate test techniques to mitigate the risk

Question 6

One of the backlogs user stories is about customers accessing the system on different browsers. This story relates to which of the quality risk category?

Answer:

A. Performance

B. Security

C. Functional

D. Compatibility

Question 7

Which of the following question from tester during the poker planning is LEAST relevant for the estimation process?

Answer:

A. "What business benefit does this story deliver?"

B. "What is the worst thing that could happen with this feature?"

C. "How will the end-user actually use this feature?"

D. "What is the business priority for this user story?"

Question 8

Which of the following information is LEAST important for the estimation of a user story?

Answer:

A. Complexity of the user story

B. Risk level of the user story

C. Development and testing effort for the user story

D. Sprint length

Question 9

The legacy core banking system is replaced by a new system so the overall system performance can be improved along with minor changes. Which of the following would serve as a test basis in addition to the user stories?

i. Experience in testing the legacy system.

ii. Performance metrics from the legacy system.

iii. Architecture diagrams from the legacy system.

iv. Customer profiles from the legacy system.

v. Defects list from the legacy system.

Answer:

A. i, ii, iv, v

B. i, ii, iii, v

C. iii, iv, v

D. All of the above

Question 10

Which of the following acceptance criteria is untestable?

Answer:

A. Performance test: The system main page should open in less than 2 seconds

B. Usability test: The data entry screen shall have a tabbing sequence to navigate from top to bottom and left to right

C. Recoverability test: The system should recover from backup within 30 seconds time after failures

D. Usability test: The system shall be user-friendly

Question 11

For the following User Story

"As a bank teller, I can search a customer based on the name, address or date of birth".

Which of the following can be considered as relevant acceptance test cases?

i. The search should be completed within a reasonable time

ii. Enter the name, address and click the Search button

iii. Enter the date of birth and click the Search button

iv. Search operation should be easy for the bank teller

Answer:

A. i, ii, iv

B. ii, iii, iv

C. ii, iii

D. All of the above

Question 12

Given the following user story:

Calculate the reward points for the gold card customer based on the following criteria:

- No reward points for shopping under $100 in one transaction
- 20 Reward points for shopping for $100 or more but less than $500 in one transaction
- 50 Reward points for shopping for $500 or more in one transaction

Which of the following black box test design technique will be BEST for testing the user story?

Answer:

A. Equivalence partitioning

B. Decision tables

C. State Transition testing

D. Use Case Testing

Question 13

Which of the following TWO approaches are correct with respect to Exploratory testing in Agile projects?

A. In Exploratory testing, testers do the risk analysis and test the critical things the tester and user think could go wrong

B. In Exploratory testing, testers test based on the model of how software should behave.

C. In Exploratory testing, testers write the detailed test cases before the test and use that for testing the system

D. In Exploratory testing, testers purely do testing based on their intuition.

Question 14

One of the Agile teams is not able to finish all the test activities as the test environment is shared for both functional and non-functional testing. Which of the following tool is most suitable for this situation?

Answer:

A. Configuration management tool

B. ALM

C. Test execution tool

D. Virtualization tools

Question 15

An Agile team is looking for a tool that can be used to build and share a knowledge base for various aspects of the project for the team members. Which of the following suits that purpose?

Answer:

A. ALM

B. Task boards

C. Wiki

D. Mind Maps

Question 16

Session-based testing is applicable for which of the following testing?

Answer:

A. Unit testing

B. System testing

C. User Acceptance testing

D. Exploratory Testing

Question 17

Which of the following will be suitable to support the Test-Driven Development (TDD) approach for the Agile team?

Answer:

A. Test design tool

B. Test execution tool

C. Test data preparation tool

D. Test case management tool

Question 18

An agile team is looking for a tool to support rapid change of business work products without losing historical data. Which of the following is suitable for this purpose?

Answer:

A. Configuration management tool

B. Task management tool

C. Test case management tool

D. Test data preparation tool

3.8 Quiz Answers

1	2	3	4	5	6	7	8	9	10	11	12	13	14	15	16	17	18
B	A	A	B	D	D	D	D	D	D	B	A	A, B	D	C	D	B	A

Question 1

FA-3.1.1 (K1) Recall the concepts of test-driven development, acceptance test-driven development and behavior-driven development

Justification:

A. Incorrect – This is true for Acceptance Test-Driven Development.

B. **Correct** – This is false. In Test-Driven Development (TDD) focus of the test is based on developer's perspective

C. Incorrect – This is true of Acceptance Test-Driven Development.

D. Incorrect – This is true of Acceptance Test-Driven Development.

Question 2

FA-3.1.2 (K1) Recall the concepts of the test pyramid

Justification:

A. **Correct** – The concept of Test Pyramid is based on testing and removing defects early

B. Incorrect.

C. Incorrect.

D. Incorrect.

Question 3

FA-3.1.3 (K2) Summarize the testing quadrants and their relationships with testing levels and testing types

Justification:

1. This is true.
2. This is false.
3. This is true.
4. This is false.

Thus:

A. **Correct**.
B. Incorrect.
C. Incorrect.
D. Incorrect.

Question 4

FA-3.1.4 For a given Agile project, practice the role of a tester in a Scrum team

Justification:

i. This is done by the tester in sprint zero
ii. This is done during the iterations, not in sprint zero
iii. This is done by the tester in sprint zero
iv. This is done by the tester in sprint zero

Thus:

A. Incorrect.
B. **Correct**.
C. Incorrect.
D. Incorrect.

Question 5

FA-3.2.1 Assess product quality risks within an Agile project

Justification:

A. Incorrect - This is true, this is done when the team is assessing each identified risk items.

B. Incorrect - This is true, this is done when the team is assessing each identified risk items.

C. Incorrect - This is true, this is done when the team is assessing each identified risk items.

D. **Correct** -This is false, this is done while defining the tests.

Question 6

FA-3.2.1 Assess product quality risks within an Agile project

Justification:

A. Incorrect.

B. Incorrect.

C. Incorrect.

D. **Correct** - This is to make sure that the system is compatible with different browsers.

Question 7

FA-3.2.2 Estimate testing effort based on iteration content and product quality risks

Justification:

A. Incorrect – This is relevant. This will help in deciding the business problem this story is solving which will result in a better testing effort estimation.

B. Incorrect – This is relevant. This will help in deciding the risk and the effort of testing required to cover the risk.

C. Incorrect – This is relevant. This will help in deciding the testing effort and can be useful for the estimation.

D. **Correct** – This is not relevant. The business priority of the user story will not help in estimating the user story.

Question 8

FA-3.2.2 Estimate testing effort based on iteration content and product quality risks

Justification:

A. Incorrect – This is relevant for estimation.

B. Incorrect – This is relevant for estimation.

C. Incorrect – This is relevant for estimation.

D. **Correct** – This is not relevant. Sprint length does not play any role in story estimation.

Question 9

FA-3.3.1 (K3) Interpret relevant information to support testing activities

Justification:

i. This is helpful to understand the application and write test cases

ii. This is helpful to define the performance baseline

iii. This is helpful to understand the application and write test cases

iv. This is helpful to write test cases

v. This is helpful during the risk analysis phase

Thus:

A. Incorrect.

B. Incorrect.

C. Incorrect.

D. **Correct**.

Question 10

FA-3.3.2 (K2) Explain to business stakeholders how to define testable acceptance criteria

Justification:

A. Incorrect – This is a valid example of the performance test.
B. Incorrect – This is a valid example of the usability test.
C. Incorrect – This is a valid example of the non-functional test.
D. **Correct** – This is not a valid example. Definition of "User-friendly" needed to test this.

Question 11

FA-3.3.3 (K3) Given a user story, write acceptance test-driven development test cases

Justification:

i. Incorrect – "within a reasonable time" is not a valid acceptance criteria
ii. **Correct** – This test is specific to search using customer name, address or date of birth.
iii. **Correct** – This test is specific to search using customer name, address or date of birth
iv. **Correct**- This test is specific to check the bank code and bank account number

Thus:

A. Incorrect.
B. **Correct**.
C. Incorrect.
D. Incorrect.

Question 12

FA-3.3.4 (K3) For both functional and non-functional behavior, write test cases using black box test design techniques based on given user stories

Justification:

A. **Correct** – Equivalence partitioning (EP) is the best option when testing different partitions.

B. Incorrect.

C. Incorrect.

D. Incorrect.

Question 13

FA-3.3.5 (K3) Perform exploratory testing to support the testing of an Agile project

Justification:

A. **Correct** – This is true for exploratory testing.

B. **Correct** – This is true for exploratory testing.

C. Incorrect – Test cases are not written for exploratory testing.

D. Incorrect – It is not just based on the intuition there is a plan required for exploratory testing.

Question 14

FA-3.4.1 (K1) Recall different tools available to testers according to their purpose and to activities in Agile projects

Justification:

A. Incorrect – Configuration management (CM) tools are suitable for providing traceability between versions of software and the tests used.

B. Incorrect - ALM tool provides visibility into the current state of the application, especially with distributed teams.

C. Incorrect – Test execution tool is useful to support test first approaches but is not related to the test environment.

D. **Correct** – Virtualization tools can be used to create multiple instances of environment for different test purposes.

Question 15

FA-3.4.1 (K1) Recall different tools available to testers according to their purpose and to activities in Agile projects

Justification:

A. Incorrect – An ALM tool provides visibility into the current state of the application but is not suitable for sharing knowledge base.

B. Incorrect – Task boards are used to visually track the task carried out by different team members and the status of user stories.

C. **Correct**- Wiki allows teams to build a knowledge base on tools and techniques for development and testing activities.

D. Incorrect – Mind maps are suitable to design the test cases and ensure the coverage.

Question 16

Agile Extension-Term (K1)

Justification:

A. Incorrect – see (D) for the correct answer.

B. Incorrect – see (D) for the correct answer.

C. Incorrect – see (D) for the correct answer.

D. **Correct** – A Session-based test management method is used for Exploratory testing.

Question 17

FA-3.4.1 (K1) Recall different tools available to testers according to their purpose and to activities in Agile projects

Justification:

A. Incorrect – Test design tool is useful to design the test cases and ensure the coverage.

B. **Correct** – Test execution tool is useful to support Test Driven Development (TDD) approach.

C. Incorrect – Test data preparation tool is useful for creating data for testing purposes.

D. Incorrect – Test case management tool is useful for managing the test cases for different phases.

Question 18

FA-3.4.1 (K1) Recall different tools available to testers according to their purpose and to activities in Agile projects

Justification:

A. **Correct** – Configuration management tool is useful to design the test cases and ensure the coverage.

B. Incorrect – Task management tool is useful to manage different tasks throughout each sprint.

C. Incorrect – Test case management tool is useful for managing the test cases for different phases.

D. Incorrect- Test data preparation tool is useful for creating data for testing purposes.

4 Sample Exam

Question 1

Which of the following tests form the foundation layer of the 'Test Pyramid'?

Answer:

a) Unit/component tests
b) System level tests.
c) Integration level tests
d) Acceptance level tests

Question 2

Which of the following is BEST to measure the Agile team's progress against the estimates?

Answer:

a) Test Status reports
b) Burndown charts
c) Agile task boards
d) Test Summary report

Question 3

Match the following terms (1-3) on the top with their corresponding best Agile software development(i-iii) on the bottom.

1. Pair programming, test-first programming
2. backlog, sprints
3. work-in-progress limit, lead time

i. Kanban

ii. Extreme Programming (XP)

iii. Scrum

Answer:

a) 1-i, 2-iii, 3-ii

b) 1-i, 2-ii, 3-iii

c) 1-ii, 2-iii, 3-i

d) 1-iii, 2-ii, 3-i

Question 4

The Agile team is working on a new project to create a mobile interface for an existing web-based application.

A few of the features are not supported in the mobile interface and the way a user can access the interface is also changing and will be documented in user stories.

Based on this information, and in addition to the user stories, which of the following would best provide relevant information to support the testing activities?

i. Existing functions, features, and quality characteristics of the web-based application

ii. Architecture diagrams for the web-based application.

iii. Obsolete user access test cases for the web-based application.

iv. Performance metrics for the existing application.

v. Defects from existing and previous releases of the web-based application.

Answer:

a) i, ii, iii, iv

b) i, ii, v

c) ii, iv, v

d) All of the above

Question 5

In the final days of the sprint, test execution is blocked due to a test environment related issue which is escalated to the environment team. Which of the following is the BEST action point from Tester's point of view in this situation?

Answer:

a) The tester can use the downtime to start working on test case preparation for stories that can be included as a part of next sprint.

b) The tester should communicate this in the daily stand-up meeting as a blocker for testing so the team can help resolve the issue or look for alternative solutions to finish testing.

c) The tester can use the environment downtime to work on automation activities.

d) The tester should document this so this can be raised in the retrospective as the area of improvement.

Question 6

Which of the following is NOT a benefit of early feedback?

a) It helps to avoid requirements misunderstandings.

b) It helps to clarify customers' requests.

c) It helps in the early discovery and resolution of bugs.

d) It helps in reducing project costs as less testing is required.

Question 7

Which of the following TWO are examples of testable acceptance criteria for test-related activities?

Select TWO options.

Answer:

a) 100% of decision coverage tested.

b) A good percentage of the functional test is automated.

c) The user access is revoked after the non-activity of account.

d) The application is responding in less than 2 sec.

Question 8

Who is responsible for the quality of the product in Agile projects?

Answer:

a) It is the responsibility of testers as they are testing the product before it reaches the real customer.

b) It is the responsibility of developers as they develop the product based on the requirements.

c) It is the responsibility of the business analysts as they draft the acceptance criteria for the product.

d) It is the responsibility of the whole team.

e) It is the responsibility of the product owner as they specify the customer requirements to the team.

Question 9

"Test automation is important to manage regression risk in Agile projects" Which of the following TWO reasons support the above statement?

i. It helps to eliminate regression risk due to high code churn

ii. It helps to ensure that all previous iterations stories are tested.

iii. It helps to receive immediate feedback on overall product quality.

iv. It helps the team to make changes to previously delivered features to meet the customer's needs.

v. It helps the team to spend more time on the current iteration activities.

Answer:

a) i and ii

b) iv and v

c) iii and iv

d) ii and v

Question 10

Which of the following supports the whole team approach in Agile development?

Answer:

a) Daily stand-up meeting
b) Continuous integration
c) Test-Driven development
d) Pairing

Question 11

Which of the following is MOST effective in reducing regression risk which is caused due to high code churn in Agile projects?

Answer:

a) Automation for test data generation
b) Automation for unit tests
c) Automation for comparing data outputs
d) Automation for restoring test environment

Question 12

The term "velocity" refers to which of the following?

Answer:

a) A Velocity chart shows the sum of estimates of the work delivered across iterations; this may be used while selecting the stories for the next iteration
b) A Velocity chart shows the degree to which the source code of a program is tested by a particular test. This may be used to show the code coverage
c) A Velocity chart shows the count of the number of defects discovered during a given period. This may be used as a criterion for stopping the testing.
d) A Velocity chart shows the number of source code changes per iteration; this may be used to know the code coverage

Question 13

Which of the following TWO activities the testers are involved in during iteration planning?

1. Discuss the Test approach and test plan with the team.
2. Help the team to break down user stories into smaller and more detailed tasks.
3. Estimate testing tasks generated by new features planned for this iteration.
4. Support the clarification of the user stories and ensure that they are testable.

Answer:

a) 1 and 4

b) 2 and 3

c) 2 and 4

d) 1 and 3

Question 14

Which of the following statements about Behavior-Driven Development (BDD) is FALSE?

Answer:

a) BDD allows a developer to focus on testing the code based on the expected behavior of the software.

b) BDD allows the developer to collaborate with other stakeholders, including testers, to define accurate unit tests focused on business needs.

c) In BDD, automated test cases are created before coding starts.

d) The result of BDD is test classes used by the developer to develop test cases

Question 15

Which of the following are required from a tester working on Agile projects?

i. Competent in test automation
ii. Competent in alpha/ beta testing
iii. Competent in experience-based testing
iv. Competent in black box testing

Answer:

a) i, ii and iii
b) i, ii, iii and iv
c) i and iii
d) i, iii and iv

Question 16

Which of the following is NOT a test related organization risk which Agile organizations may encounter?

Answer:

a) Testers work so closely with developers that they lose the appropriate tester mindset.
b) Testers become tolerant about inefficient, ineffective, or low-quality practices within the team.
c) Testers cannot keep pace with the incoming changes in time-constrained iterations.
d) Testers providing feedback on process quality.

Question 17

The tester is using the concept of testing quadrants so that the team can understand the purpose of all the test types and test levels included in the development lifecycle.

Which of the following tester statements about testing quadrants is true?

Answer:

a) Quadrant Q1 are unit level tests and Quadrant Q4 are functional tests.

b) Quadrant Q1 are unit level tests and Quadrant Q4 are user acceptance tests.

c) Quadrant Q3 are performance tests and Quadrant Q4 are functional tests.

d) Quadrant Q2 are functional tests and Quadrant Q4 are performance tests.

Question 18

Which of the following are benefits of Continuous Integration?

1. It allows earlier detection and easier root cause analysis of integration problems and conflicting changes.
2. It gives the development team regular feedback on whether the code is working.
3. It eliminates the need for a system test after the new changes are introduced.
4. It makes the code check-in process fast.

Answer:

a) 1 and 4

b) 1 and 2

c) 2 and 4

d) 1 and 3

Question 19

In one of the projects, the Agile team is using session-based test management for exploratory testing for one of the features which involve transferring files from a front-end system to a third-party system.

During the survey session, testers have raised a few questions about what to test in the feature.

Which of the following testers' questions is NOT relevant to the discussion?

Answer:

a) Which users can initiate the file transfer?

b) What is the performance requirement for the file transfer?

c) What are the various ways the users can trigger the file transfer from the front end?

d) What are the various ways the file transfer can fail?

Question 20

Given the following user story:

"As a customer, I can update my home address using the online portal.

For all customers, the address update in the portal should take less than 5 seconds, 90% of the time"

And the associated test cases:

Test Case 1: Login as a test customer. Verify that the customer home address is updated with new details.

Test Case 2: Verify in a realistic environment that the update is taking less than 5 seconds.

Which of the TWO test quadrants would the above test cases be part of?

Answer:

a) Q1 & Q2

b) Q2 & Q3

c) Q1 & Q4

d) Q2 & Q4

Question 21

Which of the following is NOT the purpose of retrospective meetings held at the end of each iteration?

Answer:

a) To discuss the team velocity and the ways to improve it.

b) To discuss the things during the iteration which were successful.

c) To discuss the things during the iteration which can be improved

d) To discuss how to incorporate the improvements and retain success in future iterations.

Question 22

The team is implementing a new user story as part of the current sprint which has an impact on the existing functionality of the product. The testers on the team realize that this may require major changes to the existing automation scripts which are used for regression testing.

What is the best course of action for the testers to take?

Answer:

a) The testers will calculate the extra time required for scripts modification and update this to the team, so the team stops taking any new user story for the current sprint.

b) The testers will notify the team of the issue. A risk analysis is done, and the team decides what regression testing must be performed to cater to new changes introduced by the user story. The testers will update the sprint plan by adding tasks to modify the automation scripts to support the new changes.

c) The current testing tasks need to be completed first for the sprint. The testers continue with their existing sprint plan and make no changes to the automation test scripts.

d) The testers will stop what they are doing and start working on the automation script modifications and communicate with the team that any other testing work for the sprint will have to be pushed to the next iteration.

Question 23

Which of the following tasks are typically expected from a tester working in an Agile team?

i. Decide on user acceptance criteria

ii. Understanding, implementing and updating the test strategy

iii. Prepare burndown charts

iv. Configuring, using, and managing test environments and test data

v. Decide on priority to the user story

Answer:

a) i and iii

b) ii and iii

c) ii & iv

d) ii & v

Question 24

An agile team is looking for a tool to manage dashboards on product status & recording conversations. Which of the following tool will be suitable for this purpose?

a) Configuration Management (CM) tool

b) Wiki

c) Test Charter

d) Continuous Integration (CI) tool

Question 25

Which of the following statement best reflects one of the values of the Agile Manifesto?

Answer:

a) In Agile development team is expected to anticipate and welcome change throughout the life cycle.

b) In Agile development team is expected to automate all unit test cases to reduce regression testing effort.

c) In Agile development, Business representatives are expected to participate in all project activities.

d) In Agile development, the tester is expected to collaborate with the Business and developer team for testing activities.

Question 26

Which of the following is one of the purposes of a test Charter?

Answer:

a) Test Charter helps the testers in test data generation for testing

b) Test Charter guides the testers in exploratory testing

c) Test Charter provides a knowledge base on tools and techniques for development and testing activities

d) Test Charter provides a quick response about the build quality and details about code changes

Question 27

During an iteration planning meeting, the team is discussing a user story. The product owner advises that sensitive customer data is captured as part of the story and should be encrypted. The developer explains that the encryption could result in an increase in development time.

Which of the following would best represent a tester's contribution to this discussion?

Answer:

a) The tester advises that encryption will increase the testing effort as there is more development required.

b) The tester advises that the priority of the story should be increased.

c) The tester advises that more performance testing will be required for the user story.

d) The tester advises that the user story needs testable acceptance criteria for the encryption functionality.

Question 28

Which of the following TWO statements are TRUE with respect to exploratory testing?

1. Exploratory testing encompasses concurrent learning, test design, and execution.
2. Exploratory testing is generally carried out by the Scrum Master in Agile projects.
3. Exploratory test cases should be automated for maximum benefit.
4. Exploratory testers should have prior knowledge of the system under test.

Answer:

a) 1 and 4

b) 1 and 2

c) 2 and 4

d) 1 and 3

Question 29

Which of the following BEST describes a tester's contribution in a retrospective meeting?

Answer:

a) Testers should only be concerned about the test-related improvement decisions focused on test effectiveness.
b) Testers should give feedback only on the automation tasks to improve test effectiveness.
c) Testers should provide feedback on all activities conducted by the Agile team during all the completed sprints.
d) Testers should give feedback only on the development task to improve test effectiveness.

Question 30

Which of the following term is NOT related to a 'User Story' used in Scrum based projects?

Answer:

a) Story acceptance criteria.
b) Story point.
c) Story priority.
d) Story entry criteria.

Question 31

Which of the following test activities is typically done during Agile projects, but is not as common in traditional projects?

Answer:

a) Testers prepare or contribute to the test strategy to address all testing activities for the project.
b) Testers spend considerable time creating, executing and maintaining automated tests and results.
c) Testers use defect-based techniques to find defects.
d) Testers contribute to the identification of risks.

Question 32

Which of the below are the examples of Test work products used by the Agile team for testing activities?

i. Quality risk catalogues
ii. Test Results log
iii. User stories
iv. automated unit tests

Answer:

a) i and ii
b) ii and iv
c) i and iii
d) All of the above.

Question 33

In order to increase the effectiveness of testing the test manager wants to introduce Independent testing for one of the Agile teams.

Which of the following is the BEST approach?

Answer:

a) Engage the independent test team in iteration planning activities
b) Engage the independent test team in release planning activities
c) Engage the independent team for carrying out test levels that might not fit well within a sprint
d) Engage the independent test team for the automation tasks during the sprints

Question 34

Which TWO of the following activities can be performed by independent testers without losing the test independence?

1. Independent testers can work on creating and supporting test environments and data.
2. Independent testers can work on the iteration testing activities.
3. Independent testers can work as 'on-demand' testers during the final days of each sprint.
4. Independent testers can work on the iteration automation activities.

Answer:

a) 1 and 4

b) 1 and 2

c) 2 and 4

d) 1 and 3

Question 35

Which of the following is NOT an Agile Manifesto statement of values?

Answer:

a) Customer collaboration over contract negotiation

b) Responding to change over following a plan

c) Processes and tools over individuals and interactions

d) Working software over comprehensive documentation

Question 36

The Agile team is performing quality risk analysis for three user stories during the iteration planning session. Match the stories with their respective quality risk based on the information below:

User Story 1: Program to calculate the account interest information for the financial end of year statement.

User Story 2: Program to store the customer sensitive information.

User Story 3: A front end screen for the system used by senior citizens.

Answer:

a) User Story 1: Security, User Story 2: Functional, User Story 3: Usability

b) User Story 1: Functional, User Story 2: Security, User Story 3: Usability

c) User Story 1: Usability, User Story 2: Security, User Story 3: Functional

d) User Story 1: Functional, User Story 2: Usability, User Story 3: Security

Question 37

During the poker planning session, the participants have decided following story points for a particular user story.

- Developers: 5
- Product owner: 3
- Tester: 8

Which story point the team should agree on?

Answer:

a) As the developers are developing the system, the developer estimates should be considered in case of a conflict.

b) The team should hold a conversation to understand why the testers and product owner gave different story points for the work required for the story. Another round of the planning poker session should occur following that discussion.

c) As the product owner owns the system, the customers' estimates should be considered in case of a conflict

d) The poker planning sessions should continue until all estimated story points are an exact match between product owner, developers, and testers.

Question 38

Given the following User Story for an online banking feature:

"As a customer, I would like to update my daily limits for my transaction account so I can transfer up to $5000 to any other account on any given day, the limit options are $1000, $2000 & $5000"

Which of the following can be considered as relevant acceptance test cases?

i. Login as a customer, check the customer can open the transaction history page.

ii. Login as a customer, check the customer can transfer the money up to his daily limit.

iii. Login as a customer, check the customer is not able to transfer money beyond his daily limit.

iv. Login as a customer, check the daily limit dropdown have the options for $1000, $2000 & $5000.

v. Login as a customer the daily limit page should open in less than 2 seconds.

Answer:

a) i, ii, iv

b) i, iii, iv

c) ii, iv, v

d) ii, iii, iv

Question 39

Which of the following TWO statements are True?

1. Early feedback can only be achieved through continuous integration.
2. Early and frequent feedback helps manage the team better since the capability of the team is transparent to everyone.
3. Early and frequent feedback helps the team find the critical defects early in the development lifecycle.
4. Early and frequent feedback enables an Agile team to build a product that reflects what the customer wants.

Answer:

a) 1 and 4

b) 2 and 3

c) 2 and 4

d) 1 and 3

Question 40

Given the following user story:

"A System to decide on the eligibility of getting the licence is based on the following criteria:

- If driver age is less than 18 then the driver is not eligible for licence
- If driver age is between 18 and 20 & driver has completed training, then the driver is eligibility for licence
- If driver age is between 18 and 20 & driver has not completed training, then the driver is not eligible for licence
- If the driver age is greater than 20 then driver training does not matter for licence eligibility

Which of the following is the best black box test design technique for the user story?

Answer:

a) State Transition testing

b) Decision tables

c) Boundary Value Analysis

d) Use Case Testing.

Answers

Correct Answers and cognitive levels

1	A	K1
2	B	K2
3	C	K1
4	C	K3
5	B	K2
6	D	K2
7	A, D	K2
8	D	K2
9	B	K2
10	A	K2
11	B	K2
12	A	K1
13	B	K1
14	C	K1
15	D	K2
16	D	K2
17	D	K2
18	B	K2
19	B	K3
20	D	K2

21	A	K2
22	B	K3
23	C	K2
24	B	K1
25	A	K1
26	B	K1
27	D	K3
28	A	K1
29	C	K2
30	D	K1
31	B	K2
32	A	K2
33	C	K2
34	D	K2
35	C	K1
36	B	K3
37	B	K3
38	D	K3
39	C	K2
40	B	K3

5 Sample Exam - Answer Sheet

Question 1

Which of the following tests form the foundation layer of the 'Test Pyramid'?

a) Unit/component tests

b) System level tests.

c) Integration level tests

d) Acceptance level tests

FA-3.1.2 (K1) Recall the concepts of the test pyramid

Justification:

a) Correct – The test levels from the base of the pyramid to the top are unit/component, integration, system, and acceptance.

b) Incorrect – see (A) for the correct answer.

c) Incorrect – see (A) for the correct answer.

d) Incorrect – see (A) for the correct answer.

Question 2

Which of the following is BEST to measure the Agile team's progress against the estimates?

a) Test Status reports

b) Burndown charts

c) Agile task boards

d) Test Summary report

FA-2.2.1 (K2) Describe the tools and techniques used to communicate the status of testing in an Agile project, including test progress and product quality

Justification:

a) Incorrect – The Test status report shows the progress of testing and can be used to measure the progress of testing but not the progress against the estimates.

b) Correct – Burndown charts show the planned progress and release date together with the actual progress of the user stories.

c) Incorrect – Task boards provide the team's current status, including the status of testing not the progress against the estimates

d) Incorrect – The Test Summary report contains a summary of test activities and final test results but not the progress against the estimates.

Question 3

Match the following terms (1-3) on the top with their corresponding best Agile software development(i-iii) on the bottom.

1. Pair programming, test-first programming
2. backlog, sprints
3. work-in-progress limit, lead time

i. Kanban
ii. Extreme Programming (XP)
iii. Scrum

a) 1-i, 2-iii, 3-ii
b) 1-i, 2-ii, 3-iii
c) 1-ii, 2-iii, 3-i
d) 1-iii, 2-ii, 3-i

FA-1.2.1 (K1) Recall Agile software development approaches

Justification:

a) Incorrect – See (C) for the correct answer.
b) Incorrect – See (C) for the correct answer
c) Correct – Pair programming, test-first programming are primary practices for XP backlog, sprints are the instruments & practices for scrum. work-in-progress limit, lead time are the instruments for Kanban.
d) Incorrect – See (C) for the correct answer

Question 4

The Agile team is working on a new project to create a mobile interface for an existing web-based application.

A few of the features are not supported in the mobile interface and the way a user can access the interface is also changing and will be documented in user stories.

Based on this information, and in addition to the user stories, which of the following would best provide relevant information to support the testing activities?

i. Existing functions, features, and quality characteristics of the web-based application
ii. Architecture diagrams for the web-based application.
iii. Obsolete user access test cases for a web-based application.
iv. Performance metrics for an existing application.
v. Defects from existing and previous releases of the web-based application.

a) i, ii, iii, iv
b) i, ii, v
c) ii, iv, v
d) All of the above

FA-3.3.1 (K3) Interpret relevant information to support testing activities

Justification:

i. This is helpful to write the test cases
ii. This is helpful to understand the application and write test cases.
iii. This information is not helpful since user access is changing with mobile interface and new user stories have been documented.
iv. Because of the new interface, baselines should be obtained using mobile devices or defined performance requirements for this type of technology.
v. This is helpful during the risk analysis phase.

Thus:

a) Incorrect.
b) Incorrect.
c) Correct.
d) Incorrect.

Question 5

In the final days of the sprint, test execution is blocked due to a test environment related issue which is escalated to the environment team. Which of the following is the BEST action point from Tester's point of view in this situation?

a) The tester can use the downtime to start working on test case preparation for stories that can be included as a part of the next sprint.

b) The tester should communicate this in the daily stand-up meeting as a blocker for testing so the team can help resolve the issue or look for alternative solutions to finish testing.

c) The tester can use the environment downtime to work on automation activities.

d) The tester should document this so this can be raised in the retrospective as the area of improvement.

FA-2.2.1 (K2) Describe the tools and techniques used to communicate the status of testing in an Agile project, including test progress and product quality

Justification:

a) Incorrect – During the iteration the team work on the current iteration tasks, not the future iteration tasks.

b) Correct – Any issues that may block test progress should be communicated during the daily stand-up meetings so the whole team is made aware of the issue(s) and can work together to find a suitable solution(s).

c) Incorrect – Automation activities are planned in parallel to testing activities, not during downtime.

d) Incorrect- Blockers should be raised immediately in the daily stand-up meetings so they can be resolved quickly.

Question 6

Which of the following is NOT a benefit of early feedback?

a) It helps to avoid requirements misunderstandings.

b) It helps to clarify customers' requests.

c) It helps in the early discovery and resolution of bugs.

d) It helps in reducing project costs as less testing is required.

FA-1.1.3 (K2) Understand the benefits of early and frequent feedback

Justification:

a) Incorrect – This is true.

b) Incorrect – This is true.

c) Incorrect – This is true.

d) **Correct** –This is false. There may be more testing required due to frequent changes.

Question 7

Which of the following TWO are examples of testable acceptance criteria for test-related activities?

Answer:

a) 100% of decision coverage tested.

b) A good percentage of the functional test is automated.

c) The user access is revoked after the non-activity of account.

d) The application is responding in less than 2 sec.

FA-3.3.2 (K2) Explain to business stakeholders how to define testable acceptance criteria

Justification:

a) Correct – This is testable.

b) Incorrect –This is not testable; this is an ambiguous statement because the percentage is not specified.

c) Incorrect – This is not testable; the period of non-activity is not specified.

d) Correct – This is testable.

Question 8

Who is responsible for the quality of the product in Agile projects?

a) It is the responsibility of testers as they are testing the product before it reaches the real customer.

b) It is the responsibility of developers as they develop the product based on the requirements.

c) It is the responsibility of the business analysts as they draft the acceptance criteria for the product.

d) **It is the responsibility of the whole team.**

e) It is the responsibility of the product owner as they specify the customer requirements to the team.

FA-1.1.2 (K2) Understand the advantages of the whole-team approach

Justification:

a) Incorrect – Testers help the team in testing tasks, but they are not alone responsible for quality as in traditional project development methods.

b) Incorrect – Developers develop the stories and help the team in automation, but they are not alone responsible for the quality of the product.

c) Incorrect – The business analyst creates the acceptance criteria with the help of the team, but they are not alone responsible for the quality of product.

d) **Correct** - In Agile projects, quality is the responsibility of the whole team.

e) Incorrect – The Product owner represents the business and provides frequent feedback to the team, but they are not alone responsible for the quality of the product.

Question 9

"Test automation is important to manage regression risk in Agile projects" Which of the following TWO reasons support the above statement?

i. It helps to eliminate regression risk due to high code churn

ii. It helps to ensure that all previous iterations stories are tested.

iii. It helps to receive immediate feedback on overall product quality.

iv. It helps the team to make changes to previously delivered features to meet the customer's needs.

v. It helps the team to spend more time on the current iteration activities.

a) i and ii

b) iv and v

c) iii and iv

d) ii and v

FA-2.2.2 (K2) Describe the process of evolving tests across multiple iterations, and explain why test automation is important to manage regression risk in Agile projects

Justification:

i. False - Automation can reduce the regression risk but cannot guarantee to eliminate all regression risk.

ii. False - It is not feasible to automate all of the tests and it is also not possible to retest/rerun all of the test cases from all of the previous iteration.

iii. False - Automated acceptance test results can provide feedback on product quality with respect to the regression since the last build, but they do not provide the status of overall product quality.

iv. True - Automation reduces the regression test effort so the team can accept and make changes to previously delivered features to meet the customer's needs.

v. True - Automation reduces the regression test effort so the team can work on tasks from the current iteration

Thus:

a) Incorrect.

b) Correct.

c) Incorrect.

d) Incorrect.

Question 10

Which of the following supports the whole team approach in Agile development?

a) **Daily stand-up meeting**

b) Continuous integration

c) Test-Driven development

d) Pairing

FA-1.1.2 (K2) Understand the advantages of the whole-team approach

Justification:

a) **Correct** – The whole-team approach is supported through the daily stand-up meetings involving all members of the team, where work progress is communicated and any impediments to progress are highlighted.

b) Incorrect - Continuous integration is not related to the whole team approach.

c) Incorrect – Test-driven development is not related to the whole team approach.

d) Incorrect – In pairing two team members (e.g., a tester and a developer, two testers, or a tester and a product owner sit together at one workstation to perform a testing or other sprint task), but pairing does not support of the whole team approach.

Question 11

Which of the following is MOST effective in reducing regression risk which is caused due to high code churn in Agile projects?

a) Automation for test data generation

b) Automation for unit tests

c) Automation for comparing data outputs

d) Automation for restoring test environment

FA-2.2.2 (K2) Describe the process of evolving tests across multiple iterations and explain why test automation is important to manage regression risk in Agile projects

Justification:

a) Incorrect- see (B) for a detailed justification

b) Correct.

Automation unit tests will provide rapid feedback on product quality and can reduce the risk of regression. Automation for test data generation, comparing data output and restoring test environment will allow the team to spend more time developing and testing new features but will not reduce the risk of code churn.

c) Incorrect- see (B) for a detailed justification

d) Incorrect- see (B) for a detailed justification

Question 12

The term "velocity" refers to which of the following?

a) A Velocity chart shows the sum of estimates of the work delivered across iterations; this may be used while selecting the stories for the next iteration

b) A Velocity chart shows the degree to which the source code of a program is tested by a particular test. This may be used to show the code coverage

c) A Velocity chart shows the count of the number of defects discovered during a given period. This may be used as a criterion for stopping the testing.

d) A Velocity chart shows the number of source code changes per iteration; this may be used to know the code coverage

Agile Extension-Term (K1)

Justification:

a) **Correct** – This is true for the velocity chart.

b) Incorrect – This is a code coverage chart, not a velocity chart.

c) Incorrect – This is a defect discover rate chart, not a velocity chart.

d) Incorrect – This is a Code Churn chart, not a velocity chart.

Question 13

Which of the following TWO activities the testers are involved in during iteration planning?

1. Discuss the Test approach and test plan with the team.
2. Help the team to break down user stories into smaller and more detailed tasks.
3. Estimate testing tasks generated by new features planned for this iteration.
4. Support the clarification of the user stories and ensure that they are testable.

a) 1 and 4

b) 2 and 3

c) 2 and 4

d) 1 and 3

FA-1.2.5 (K1) Know the differences between iteration and release planning, and how a tester adds value to each activity

Justification:

1. False – This is expected during release planning.
2. True – This is expected during iteration planning.
3. True – This is expected during iteration planning.
4. False – This is expected during release planning.

Thus:

a) Incorrect.

b) **Correct**.

c) Incorrect.

d) Incorrect.

Question 14

Which of the following statements about Behavior-Driven Development (BDD) is FALSE?

a) BDD allows a developer to focus on testing the code based on the expected behavior of the software.

b) BDD allows the developer to collaborate with other stakeholders, including testers, to define accurate unit tests focused on business needs.

c) In BDD, automated test cases are created before coding starts.

d) The result of BDD is test classes used by the developer to develop test cases

FA-3.1.1 (K1) Recall the concepts of test-driven development, acceptance test-driven development and behavior-driven development

Justification:

a) Incorrect – This is true for BDD.

b) Incorrect – This is true for BDD.

c) Correct – This is true for TDD – not BDD.

d) Incorrect – This is true for BDD.

Question 15

Which of the following are required from a tester working on Agile projects?

i. Competent in test automation
ii. Competent in alpha/ beta testing
iii. Competent in experience-based testing
iv. Competent in black box testing

a) i, ii and iii
b) i, ii, iii and iv
c) i and iii
d) i, iii and iv

FA-2.3.1 (K2) Understand the skills (people, domain, and testing) of a tester in an Agile team

Justification:

i. This is required from a tester in Agile project. There is a lot of emphasis on automation tests, so it is an essential skill for a tester.
ii. This is not required from a tester in Agile project as Alpha/Beta testing is done by customers. Testers can assist, but it is not a necessary skill.
iii. This is required from a tester in Agile project. There is a lot of emphasis on exploratory testing, so it is an essential skill for a tester.
iv. This is required from a tester in Agile project. Testers should be competent in black box testing for both Agile and traditional projects.

Thus:

a) Incorrect.
b) Incorrect.
c) Incorrect.
d) **Correct**.

Question 16

Which of the following is NOT a test related organization risk which Agile organizations may encounter?

a) Testers work so closely with developers that they lose the appropriate tester mindset.

b) Testers become tolerant about inefficient, ineffective, or low-quality practices within the team.

c) Testers cannot keep pace with the incoming changes in time-constrained iterations.

d) Testers providing feedback on process quality.

FA-2.3.2 (K2) Understand the role of a tester within an Agile team

Justification:

a) Incorrect – This is true, Agile organizations may encounter this test related risk.

b) Incorrect – This is true, Agile organizations may encounter this test related risk.

c) Incorrect – This is true, Agile organizations may encounter this test related risk.

d) **Correct** – This is NOT a test related organization risk. This is required from an agile tester.

Question 17

The tester is using the concept of testing quadrants so that the team can understand the purpose of all the test types and test levels included in the development lifecycle.

Which of the following tester statements about testing quadrants is true?

a) Quadrant Q1 are unit level tests and Quadrant Q4 are functional tests.

b) Quadrant Q1 are unit level tests and Quadrant Q4 are user acceptance tests.

c) Quadrant Q3 are performance tests and Quadrant Q4 are functional tests.

d) Quadrant Q2 are functional tests and Quadrant Q4 are performance tests.

FA-3.1.3 (K2) Summarize the testing quadrants and their relationships with testing levels and testing types

Justification:

- Quadrant Q1 is unit level, technology facing, and supports the developers.
- Quadrant Q2 is system/functional level, business facing, and confirms product behavior
- Quadrant Q3 is user acceptance level, business facing, and contains tests that critique the product
- Quadrant Q4 is system or operational acceptance level, technology facing, and contains tests that critique the product.

Thus:

a) Incorrect.

b) Incorrect.

c) Incorrect.

d) Correct.

Question 18

Which of the following TWO are benefits of Continuous Integration?

1. It allows earlier detection and easier root cause analysis of integration problems and conflicting changes.
2. It gives the development team regular feedback on whether the code is working.
3. It eliminates the need for a system test after the new changes are introduced.
4. It makes the code check-in process fast.

a) 1 and 4

b) 1 and 2

c) 2 and 4

d) 1 and 3

FA-1.2.4 (K2) Understand the use and purpose of continuous integration

Justification:

1. This is a benefit as continuous integration finds integration problems earlier, also conflicting changes when multiple people check in code at the same time are found during the process.
2. This is a benefit as continuous integration results provide the development team feedback on their code.
3. This is not a benefit as system testing is still required after the continuous integration.
4. This is not a benefit as code check-in is actually slow after continuous integration as additional automated tests are run during the process.

Thus:

a) Incorrect.

b) **Correct**.

c) Incorrect.

d) Incorrect.

Question 19

In one of the projects, the Agile team is using session-based test management for exploratory testing for one of the features which involve transferring files from a front-end system to a third-party system.

During the survey session, testers have raised a few questions about what to test in the feature.

Which of the following testers' questions is NOT relevant to the discussion?

a) Which users can initiate the file transfer?

b) What is the performance requirement for the file transfer?

c) What are the various ways the users can trigger the file transfer from the front end?

d) What are the various ways the file transfer can fail?

FA-3.3.5 (K3) Perform exploratory testing to support the testing of an Agile project

Justification:

a) Incorrect – This is a relevant question this will help in the design and execution of exploratory tests.

b) Correct – This question is NOT relevant for exploratory testing; this is helpful to design the performance tests.

c) Incorrect – This is a relevant question; this will help in the design and execution of the exploratory tests.

d) Incorrect – This is a relevant question; this will help in the design and execution of the exploratory tests.

Question 20

Given the following user story:

“As a customer, I can update my home address using the online portal.

For all customers, the address update in the portal should take less than 5 seconds, 90% of the time”

And the associated test cases:

Test Case 1: Login as a test customer. Verify that the customer home address is updated with new details.

Test Case 2: Verify in a realistic environment that the update is taking less than 5 seconds.

Which of the TWO test quadrants would the above test cases be part of?

a) Q1 & Q2

b) Q2 & Q3

c) Q1 & Q4

d) Q2 & Q4

FA-3.1.3 (K2) Summarize the testing quadrants and their relationships with testing levels and testing types

Justification:

a) Incorrect – see below.

b) Incorrect – see below.

c) Incorrect – see below.

d) Correct –Test Case 1 is the system level which is part of Q2, and Test Case 2 is Performance test which is part of the Q4.

Question 21

Which of the following is NOT the purpose of retrospective meetings held at the end of each iteration?

a) **To discuss the team velocity and the ways to improve it.**

b) To discuss the things during the iteration which were successful.

c) To discuss the things during the iteration which can be improved

d) To discuss how to incorporate the improvements and retain success in future iterations.

FA-1.2.3 (K2) Understand how retrospectives can be used as a mechanism for process improvement in Agile projects

Justification:

a) **Correct** – The purpose of a retrospective meeting is not to discuss team velocity or ways to improve it.

b) Incorrect – True - one of the purposes of a retrospective meeting is to find out the things which were successful.

c) Incorrect – True - one of the purposes of a retrospective meeting is to find out the things which can be improved.

d) Incorrect – True - one of the purposes of a retrospective meeting is to incorporate the improvements in future iterations.

Question 22

The team is implementing a new user story as part of the current sprint which has an impact on the existing functionality of the product. The testers on the team realize that this may require major changes to the existing automation scripts which are used for regression testing.

What is the best course of action for the testers to take?

a) The testers will calculate the extra time required for scripts modification and update this to the team, so the team stops taking any new user story for the current sprint.

b) The testers will notify the team of the issue. A risk analysis is done, and the team decides what regression testing must be performed to cater to new changes introduced by the user story. The testers will update the sprint plan by adding tasks to modify the automation scripts to support the new changes.

c) The current testing tasks need to be completed first for the sprint. The testers continue with their existing sprint plan and make no changes to the automation test scripts.

d) The testers will stop what they are doing and start working on the automation script modifications and communicate with the team that any other testing work for the sprint will have to be pushed to the next iteration.

FA-3.1.4 (K3) For a given Agile project, practice the role of a tester in a Scrum team

Justification:

a) Incorrect – A risk analysis should be done including the whole team and a collaborative decision should be made.

b) Correct – The decision to modify the test scripts should be done collaboratively with the whole team. The tester is then responsible to make changes to the iteration plan as required.

c) Incorrect – The tester must notify the team who will then decide what to do with the issue.

d) Incorrect – It is not up to the tester alone to determine the scope of work. This issue will be addressed by creating a new user story or modifying an existing user story and will be addressed by the entire team during sprint planning.

Question 23

Which of the following tasks are typically expected from a tester working in an Agile team?

i. Decide on user acceptance criteria

ii. Understanding, implementing and updating the test strategy

iii. Prepare burndown charts

iv. Configuring, using, and managing test environments and test data

v. Decide on priority to the user story

a) i and iii

b) ii and iii

c) ii & iv

d) ii & v

FA-2.3.2 (K2) Understand the role of a tester within an Agile team

Justification:

i. Incorrect – This task is done collaboratively by the whole team.

ii. **Correct**– This task is typical done by the Agile tester.

iii. Incorrect – In Agile, it is the Scrum Master's role to produce and update the burndown chart from the information supplied by the rest of the team

iv. **Correct** – This task is typical done by the Agile tester.

v. Incorrect – The business users or product owner decides on the priority of user stories.

Thus:

a) Incorrect.

b) Incorrect.

c) **Correct**.

d) Incorrect.

Question 24

An agile team is looking for a tool to manage dashboards on product status & recording conversations. Which of the following tool will be suitable for this purpose?

a) Configuration Management (CM) tool

b) Wiki

c) Test Charter

d) Continuous Integration (CI) tool

FA-3.4.1 (K1) Recall different tools available to testers according to their purpose and to activities in Agile projects

Justification:

a) Incorrect – A Configuration Management (CM) tool will be suitable for storing source code and other test work products.

b) **Correct** – This is one of many purposes of a wiki tool.

c) Incorrect – A Test Charter will be suitable for exploratory testing.

d) Incorrect – A Continuous Integration (CI) tool will be suitable for visibility on build status and automatic reporting.

Question 25

Which of the following statement best reflects one of the values of the Agile Manifesto?

a) In Agile development, team is expected to anticipate and welcome change throughout the life cycle.

b) In Agile development, team is expected to automate all unit test cases to reduce regression testing effort.

c) In Agile development, Business representatives are expected to participate in all project activities.

d) In Agile development, the tester is expected to collaborate with the Business and developer team for testing activities.

FA-1.1.1 (K1) Recall the basic concept of Agile software development based on the Agile Manifesto

Justification:

a) **Correct** – In the Agile development team respond quickly to customers, product users, and the market in general throughout the life cycle. This helps to develop relevant products that people want to use.

b) Incorrect – It is normal practice in Agile development, but it is not one of the values in the Agile Manifesto.

c) Incorrect – It is normal practice in Agile development, but it is not one of the values in the Agile Manifesto.

d) Incorrect – It is normal practice in Agile development, but it is not one of the values in the Agile Manifesto.

Question 26

Which of the following is one of the purposes of a test Charter?

a) Test Charter helps the testers in test data generation for testing

b) Test Charter guides the testers in exploratory testing

c) Test Charter provides a knowledge base on tools and techniques for development and testing activities

d) Test Charter provides a quick response about the build quality and details about code changes

FA-3.4.1 (K1) Recall different tools available to testers according to their purpose and to activities in Agile projects

Justification:

a) Incorrect – This would be one of the purposes of a data generation tool

b) **Correct** – This is one of many purposes of a Test Charter.

c) Incorrect – This would be one of the purposes of a Wiki.

d) Incorrect – This would be one of the purposes of a Continuous Integration (CI) tool

Question 27

During an iteration planning meeting, the team is discussing a user story. The product owner advises that sensitive customer data is captured as part of the story and should be encrypted. The developer explains that the encryption could result in an increase in development time.

Which of the following would best represent a tester's contribution to this discussion?

a) The tester advises that encryption will increase the testing effort as there is more development required.

b) The tester advises that the priority of the story should be increased.

c) The tester advises that more performance testing will be required for the user story.

d) The tester advises that the user story needs testable acceptance criteria for the encryption functionality.

FA-1.2.2 (K3) Write testable user stories in collaboration with developers and business representatives

Justification:

a) Incorrect – It is not necessary that the increase in development effort will result in an increase in the testing effort.

b) Incorrect – The product owner decides on the priority of the story, not the tester.

c) Incorrect – Changes to performance testing requirements will be decided by the team, not the tester alone.

d) **Correct** – The tester should ensure that there are testable acceptance criteria for all of the functions of the user story.

Question 28

Which of the following TWO statements are TRUE with respect to exploratory testing?

1. Exploratory testing encompasses concurrent learning, test design, and execution.
2. Exploratory testing is generally carried out by the Scrum Master in Agile projects.
3. Exploratory test cases should be automated for maximum benefit.
4. Exploratory testers should have prior knowledge of the system under test.

a) 1 and 4

b) 1 and 2

c) 2 and 4

d) 1 and 3

Agile Extension-Term (K1)

Justification:

1. True - Exploratory testing encompasses concurrent learning, test design, and execution.
2. False -Exploratory testing is carried out by testers.
3. False - Automation of exploratory testing is not possible as test design and execution happens in parallel.
4. True - Testers need a good understanding of how the system is used and how to determine when it fails.

Thus:

a) Correct.

b) Incorrect.

c) Incorrect.

d) Incorrect.

Question 29

Which of the following BEST describes a tester's contribution in a retrospective meeting?

a) Testers should only be concerned about the test-related improvement decisions focused on test effectiveness.

b) Testers should give feedback only on the automation tasks to improve test effectiveness.

c) Testers should provide feedback on all activities conducted by the Agile team during all the completed sprints.

d) Testers should give feedback only on the development task to improve test effectiveness.

A-1.2.3 (K2) Understand how retrospectives can be used as a mechanism for process improvement in Agile projects

Justification:

a) Incorrect – see (C) for the correct answer

b) Incorrect – see (C) for the correct answer

c) **Correct** – All team members, including testers, should provide input and feedback on both testing and non-testing activities in retrospective meetings

d) Incorrect – see (C) for the correct answer

Question 30

Which of the following term is NOT related to a 'User Story' used in Scrum based projects?

a) Story acceptance criteria.

b) Story point.

c) Story priority.

d) Story entry criteria.

Agile Extension-Term (K1)

Justification:

a) Incorrect – This is related to user story, story acceptance criteria are created in collaboration by business representatives, developers, and testers for each user story.

b) Incorrect – This is related to the user story; a story point is assigned to each user story during the poker planning session.

c) Incorrect – This is related to user story; each user story is assigned a priority by the business users during release planning.

d) Correct – There is no term as story entry criteria.

Question 31

Which of the following test activities is typically done during Agile projects, but is not as common in traditional projects?

a) Testers prepare or contribute to the test strategy to address all testing activities for the project.

b) Testers spend considerable time creating, executing and maintaining automated tests and results.

c) Testers use defect-based techniques to find defects.

d) Testers contribute to the identification of risks.

FA-2.1.1 (K2) Describe the differences between testing activities in Agile projects and non-Agile projects

Justification:

a) Incorrect – This is common in both Agile and traditional projects.

b) Correct – Test automation occurs at all levels in most Agile teams. In Agile projects testers focus on automating, executing and maintaining tests on integration, system, and acceptance level. In traditional projects, testers do not have the same focus on automation.

c) Incorrect – Defect based techniques such as software attacks and error guessing are common in both Agile and traditional projects.

d) Incorrect – Testers' contribution in risk identification is common in both Agile and traditional projects.

Question 32

Which of the below are the examples of Test work products used by the Agile team for testing activities?

i. Quality risk catalogues

ii. Test Results log

iii. User stories

iv. automated unit tests

a) i and ii

b) ii and iv

c) i and iii

d) All of the above.

FA-2.1.2 (K2) Describe how development and testing activities are integrated in Agile projects

Justification:

i. This is an example of a Test work product.

ii. This is an example of a Test work product.

iii. This is an example of a business-oriented work product, not a Test work product.

iv. This is an example of a development work product, not a Test Work product.

Thus:

a) Correct.

b) Incorrect.

c) Incorrect.

d) Incorrect.

Question 33

In order to increase the effectiveness of testing the test manager wants to introduce Independent testing for one of the Agile teams.

Which of the following is the BEST approach?

a) Engage the independent test team in iteration planning activities

b) Engage the independent test team in release planning activities

c) Engage the independent team for carrying out test levels that might not fit well within a sprint

d) Engage the independent test team for the automation tasks during the sprints

FA-2.1.3 (K2) Describe the role of independent testing in Agile projects

Justification:

a) Incorrect –The testers who are working on the iteration should be engaged in iteration related activities, not the independent test team.

b) Incorrect –The testers who are working on the iteration should be engaged in release planning, not the independent test team.

c) Correct – Independent testing team can carry out test levels e.g. system integration testing, that might not fit well within a sprint

d) Incorrect – Developers and testers work collaboratively to do the automation task during the sprints

Question 34

Which TWO of the following activities can be performed by independent testers without losing the test independence?

1. Independent testers can work on creating and supporting test environments and data.
2. Independent testers can work on the iteration testing activities.
3. Independent testers can work as 'on-demand' testers during the final days of each sprint.
4. Independent testers can work on the iteration automation activities.

a) 1 and 4

b) 1 and 2

c) 2 and 4

d) 1 and 3

FA-2.1.3 (K2) Describe the role of independent testing in Agile projects

Justification:

1. Independent testers can work on iteration-independent activities like creating and supporting test environments and data **without losing test independence.**
2. Iteration testing activities need a sound understanding of the product and close collaboration with the Agile team, there is a significant risk that objectivity will be compromised because the testers are "too close" to the development team and form an unconscious bias.
3. Independent testers can provide an objective, unbiased evaluation of the software at the end of a sprint **without losing test independence**.
4. If the independent testers work on the automation testing activities with the developers, then there is a chance to lose test independence as testers are "too close" to the development team and form an unconscious bias.

Thus:

a) Incorrect

b) Incorrect

c) Incorrect

d) **Correct**.

Question 35

Which of the following is NOT an Agile Manifesto statement of values?

a) Customer collaboration over contract negotiation

b) Responding to change over following a plan

c) Processes and tools over individuals and interactions

d) Working software over comprehensive documentation

FA-1.1.1 (K1) Recall the basic concept of Agile software development based on the Agile Manifesto

Justification:

The Manifesto consists of 4 key values:

- Individuals and interactions over processes and tools;
- Working software over comprehensive documentation;
- Customer collaboration over contract negotiation;
- Responding to change over following a plan

Thus:

a) Incorrect.

b) Incorrect.

c) **Correct**.

d) Incorrect.

Question 36

The Agile team is performing quality risk analysis for three user stories during the iteration planning session. Match the stories with their respective quality risk based on the information below:

- **User Story 1**: Program to calculate the account interest information for the financial end of year statement.
- **User Story 2:** Program to store the customer sensitive information.
- **User Story 3**: A front end screen for the system used by senior citizens.

a) User Story 1: Security, User Story 2: Functional, User Story 3: Usability

b) User Story 1: Functional, User Story 2: Security, User Story 3: Usability

c) User Story 1: Usability, User Story 2: Security, User Story 3: Functional

d) User Story 1: Functional, User Story 2: Usability, User Story 3: Security

FA-3.2.1 (K3) Assess product quality risks within an Agile project

Justification:

- **User Story 1**: Calculation (accuracy) in the report is a functional risk.
- **User Story 2**: Storing customer sensitive information is a security risk.
- **User Story 3**: Difficulty in understanding screens for users (senior citizens) is a usability risk.

a) Incorrect.

b) Correct.

c) Incorrect.

d) Incorrect.

Question 37

During the poker planning session, the participants have decided following story points for a particular user story.

- Developers: 5
- Product owner: 3
- Testers: 8

Which story point the team should agree on?

a) As the developers are developing the system, the developer estimates should be considered in case of a conflict.

b) The team should hold a conversation to understand why the testers and product owner gave different story points for the work required for the story. Another round of the planning poker session should occur following that discussion.

c) As the product owner owns the system, the customers' estimates should be considered in case of a conflict

d) The poker planning sessions should continue until all estimated story points are an exact match between product owner, developers, and testers.

FA-3.2.2 (K3) Estimate testing effort based on iteration content and product quality risks

Justification:

a) Incorrect – The entire team must agree on the estimate for the user story. The developer alone does not understand the complexity of developing or testing the functionality.

b) Correct – Conversation is required to understand why there is a mismatch. After that the planning poker sessions should continue for the user story until the entire team is satisfied with the estimated effort.

c) Incorrect – The entire team must agree on the estimate for the user story. The customer alone does not understand the complexity of developing or testing the functionality.

d) Incorrect – It is not necessary that they match, a rule could be made that the highest estimate is taken, or an average taken of all three estimates. This is up to the team to decide before the planning poker session.

Question 38

Given the following User Story for an online banking feature:

"As a customer, I would like to update my daily limits for my transaction account so I can transfer up to $5000 to any other account on any given day, the limit options are $1000, $2000 & $5000"

Which of the following can be considered as relevant acceptance test cases?

i. Login as a customer, check the customer can open the transaction history page.
ii. Login as a customer, check the customer can transfer the money up to his daily limit.
iii. Login as a customer, check the customer is not able to transfer money beyond his daily limit.
iv. Login as a customer, check the daily limit dropdown have the options for $1000, $2000 & $5000.
v. Login as a customer the daily limit page should open in less than 2 seconds.

a) i, ii, iv
b) i, iii, iv
c) ii, iv, v
d) ii, iii, iv

FA-3.3.3 (K3) Given a user story, write acceptance test-driven development test cases

Justification:

i. Incorrect – User story is specific to customers' daily limit change, not the transaction history.
ii. **Correct** – This test is specific to a customer and results in verifying the daily limit functionality is working fine.
iii. **Correct** – This test is specific to a customer and results in verifying the daily limit functionality is working fine.
iv. **Correct** -This test is specific to a customer and results in verifying the daily limit is set up correctly in the system.
v. Incorrect – User story does not mention performance requirements.

Thus:

a) Incorrect.
b) Incorrect.
c) Incorrect.
d) Correct.

Question 39

Which of the following TWO statements are True?

1. Early feedback can only be achieved through continuous integration.
2. Early and frequent feedback helps manage the team better since the capability of the team is transparent to everyone.
3. Early and frequent feedback helps the team find the critical defects early in the development lifecycle.
4. Early and frequent feedback enables an Agile team to build a product that reflects what the customer wants.

a) 1 and 4

b) 2 and 3

c) 2 and 4

d) 1 and 3

FA-1.1.3 (K2) Understand the benefits of early and frequent feedback

Justification:

1. Incorrect – Continuous integration is one way to provide early feedback not the only way.
2. **Correct** – Early feedback makes it easy to check the work done in an iteration and see how it can be improved.
3. Incorrect – Early feedback helps in finding the defects early but not necessarily the critical defects.
4. **Correct** – Early feedback helps the customers to indicate if requirements are not met and modify functionality if required.

Thus:

a) Incorrect.

b) Incorrect.

c) Correct.

d) Incorrect.

Question 40

Given the following user story:

"A System to decide on the eligibility of getting the licence is based on the following criteria:

- If the driver age is less than 18 then driver is not eligible for licence
- If driver age is between 18 and 20 & driver has completed training, then the driver is eligibility for licence
- If driver age is between 18 and 20 & driver has not completed training, then driver is not eligible for licence
- If the driver age is greater than 20 then driver training does not matter for licence eligibility

Which of the following is the best black box test design technique for the user story?

a) State Transition testing

b) Decision tables

c) Boundary Value Analysis

d) Use Case Testing.

FA-3.3.4 (K3) For both functional and non-functional behavior, write test cases using black-box test design techniques based on given user stories

Justification:

a) Incorrect – see (B) for the correct answer.

b) Correct – Decision tables are best for user stories where the Actions are based on the Conditions.

c) Incorrect – see (B) for correct answer.

d) Incorrect – see (B) for the correct answer.

Printed in Poland
by Amazon Fulfillment
Poland Sp. z o.o., Wrocław

86783996R30125